Joy Cometh
in the Morning

Joy Cometh
in the Morning

Leary E. Bonnett

Amazing Grace
Publications

Published by:
Amazing Grace Publications, Inc
P.O. Box 69
Brooklyn, NY 11215

Copyright © 2005 Leary E. Bonnett
Interior text design by Tom Davis

ISBN: 0-9-713277-1-8
Library of Congress Control Number: 2005924498

Joy Cometh in the Morning.

First Edition
Printed and bound in the United States of America by Morris Publishing • www.morrispublishing.com • 800-650-7888
1 2 3 4 5 6 7 8 9 10

This book is dedicated to Chief Rufus B. Ufondu and his beloved wife, Beatrice Ufondu and the entire Ufondu clan at Oraifite, Anambra State, Nigeria, West Africa.

Chief Rufus B. Ufondu (left)
Ms. Beatrice Ufondu (center)

Acknowledgement

ꙮ

I EXPERIENCED A SPECIAL benediction writing
this book, but I make no claim that it is any way a
masterpiece. I view it instead as a small token of appre-
ciation to a wonderful family that reminded me of the
sacred responsibility of the biblical writer who exhorts,
"Train up a child in the way that he should go and
when he is old he will not depart from it (Proverbs
22:6).

In December 2004, my wife Terry-Jan Blackett-
Bonnett, M.D., our young son Harun Ibrahim, my wife's
aunt, Patricia Layne and I, embarked on a two week
Christmas vacation to the Ibo country in Eastern Nigeria. We were the guests of Dr. Solibe Ufondu, M.D. and
his wife Dr. Uchenna Ufondu, M.D., colleagues of my
wife in the medical profession.

During our sojourn at the Ufondu compound in
Oraifite, Anambra State, we celebrated the tenth year

wedding anniversary of Drs. Solibe and Uchenna. It was a festive affair accompanied by tribal dancers and unlimited food and drink. During our stay in Africa, we were additionally blessed with the special privilege of sharing Christmas dinner at the residence of the State Governor, Dr. Chris Ngige, M.D. and to attend other memorable events that will forever be enshrined within our memories. However, what remained in my estimation the most important daily event that I experienced during our two-week stay was the fact that the Ufondu family began each day with family devotions.

Every morning at five O'clock, Beatrice Ufondu, the devoted wife of the ninety-five year old Chief would go through the elaborate compound ringing a bell, summoning everyone to morning devotions. Within a short period of time, family members, guests and the house help, with sleep still heavy on their eyes, assembled in the spacious living room. At this location morning devotions were conducted in the Ibo language, accompanied by songs and readings from the Ibo Bible. The sessions were vibrant and full of praise to Almighty God and were the perfect way to start the day.

I took special note of the fact that on those occasions when any of the other brothers arrived home even in the wee hours of the morning, they still presented themselves for morning devotions at the five O'clock ringing of Beatrice's bell. Even on our way back to the USA when we stayed from a brief while at Sir Uzo

Ufondu's residence in Lagos, one of Chief Ufondu's sons, we were summoned to morning devotions with his family. The practice instilled at Oraifite took root and remains with each family member in their respective households, testifying to the fact that spiritual values instilled during childhood inevitably remains with someone throughout their lifetime.

The example of the Ufondu family is the inoculation for so many of the ills that beset our world at large, that being, that so many of life's battles are won in the early mornings when people offer up their circumstances to God, requesting that He order their steps throughout the day. This was the example of our Lord and it is a fitting way for us to order our own lives.

Reverend Leary E. Bonnett
Brooklyn, New York

Foreword

❦

THIS INSIGHTFUL TREATISE is a testament to the oft-forgotten truth that in God's economy suffering never has the last word. With skillful insight and execution, Reverend Leary E. Bonnett revisits biblical narratives bearing witness to the fact that God is not only a God for us, but also a God with us.

Throughout the arresting chapters, the author skillfully brings home the reality that God continues to pitch his tent in the midst of humanity. If and when we develop the courage to reach out like the woman with the issue of blood and touch the hem of our Lord's garment, or position ourselves at His feet like Mary Magdalene did when she wet his feet with tears and wiped them with her hair and anointed them with expensive ointment, we might discover that He is prepared to reach back and heal us in body, mind and spirit.

We are also reminded that even though we might be subjected to harrowing episodes of suffering, which at times threaten to derange a person's mind, we must struggle at all costs to discover meaning for our lives, despite the magnitude of suffering to which we might be subjected. Honesty impels us to admit that this is no easy task. However, it is the way that suffering is faced that makes the difference whether pain, sorrow, difficulty, deprivation, or challenge, becomes part of our soul's stretching or shrinking. The author in no way trivializes suffering and admits that it is oftentimes painful. However, he does send home the message that rather than allowing suffering to define and rule our existence, we are afforded the sacred opportunity of calling upon a force field beyond our suffering with the capability of transforming our experiences. Grounded in such goodness, we are afforded supernatural energies to grapple with any adversity, because we draw on the grace of a world much larger than suffering.

Reverend Bonnett is a megaphone testifying to the world that the Christian message would in no way shield us from the painful scrapes of life, but by individually taking up our cross we can encounter God in the midst of our suffering. When we come into God's presence as sufferers, we are afforded the opportunity to learn who we are, in our suffering and beyond our suffering. By the same token, we might learn who God is. We might become intimately acquainted with the

God who suffers and the God who both transcends and transforms suffering.

Terry – Jan Blackett – Bonnett, M.D.
Brooklyn, New York

Contents

Chapter One

Hold On To the Hem
(Mark 5-25-34)

❧❦

The story of the woman with the issue of blood is one of the best-known miracles of Jesus to be recorded in the Bible. It is an enchanting episode with a universal appeal all its own. So much so, that individuals possessing a mere rudimentary knowledge of biblical events are somehow strangely familiar with the details of the timeless drama that continues to captivate the imagination of untold millions down throughout the ages. Each of the three of the Synoptic Gospels — Matthew, Mark and Luke, bear witness to the occurrence of the supernatural event. However, it is Mark's rendering of the report that tends to amplify the bare-boned details of the poor woman's plight.

What makes the account so intriguing is not simply because God orchestrated a transformation in the circumstances of a life-battered soul. But more importantly, when the woman's back was literally against the wall and she found herself confronted by what appeared to be insurmountable odds, she unleashed the kind of faith that enabled her to visualize life as something worth preserving. By so doing, she continued to weave the tattered threads of a broken existence into a firm pattern of meaning and responsibility.

At a time when the average individual might have thrown up their hands in frustration and surrendered to their circumstances, the undeterred struggler dug her heels in the sand and defiantly stood her ground until she experienced a change in her situation.

When we throw the searchlight of scrutiny on the core details of the alluring case history, it simply boggles the mind that the beleaguered sufferer mustered the courage to retain a spiritual grip on an uncertain future. But, maybe that is the very reason why we find her story so captivating. Despite the fact that she was assailed by an avalanche of adversity, she did not collapse under the enormous weight of oppression and give up the fight. But instead, she refused to wave the white flag of surrender and call it quits by summoning the resources needed to transcend her crippling circumstances and latched on to a spiritual wavelength that resonated with the vibratory frequency of God's resurrection possibilities.

The medical diagnosis indicates that for twelve long years the woman was inflicted with an "issue of blood." The language employed by the biblical writer is cloaked in political correctness. However, when we unpack the statement in the vernacular of the medical establishment, it translates into the reality that she experienced a malfunction in her female reproduction system that induced incessant bleeding or hemorrhaging, for twelve pain-wracked years.

The narrative indicates that for the duration of her tribulation, "she suffered many things of many physicians" and spent all that she had and was nothing bettered, but rather grew worse. The language employed on this second occasion indicates that when she was confronted by life-threatening circumstances, she feverishly traversed her local community and repeatedly placed herself under the care of one physician after another, hoping against all odds that she would someday discover a cure for her malady. During her plight of desperation she might very well have submitted herself to clinical trials conducted by the leading specialists of her day, only to discover that potential remedies administered by the skilled practitioners simply did not garner the expected results.

In her frail condition, she undoubtedly suffered bouts of anemia and experienced sleepless nights brought about by constant pain that throbbed annoyingly at her body, robbing her of much needed sleep. There is also a high probability that she experienced near-death experiences precipitated by excessive blood loss that continuously sapped her energy and weakened her fragile frame. Adding insult to injury, after spending all of her hard-earned money she was rendered broke and penniless.

The day finally arrived when her most recent physician presented her with the dreadful prognosis that no human ear is ever really prepared to hear: "I am sorry madam, but there is nothing more that I could do for you." Shocked and saddened by the grim pronouncement, she was unceremoniously discharged from treatment as an incurable case and sent home to die. With the black flag of death fluttering menacingly on the horizon, a sinister and unkind hand appeared to be pulling down the curtains of life on the poor sister, who for twelve years was subjected to enormous pain and privation.

After being discharged with such a depressing report, the average individual would undoubtedly become diligent in putting their personal affairs in order. In all likelihood, they would recognize the remaining days of their mortal existence as the opportune time to become engaged in mending broken relationships with family members and friends with whom they had become estranged at some point over the past years. More importantly, they would realize the imperative of making peace with their Creator before embarking on their initiation into eternity.

While the life experiences of the suffering woman appeared to be conspiring to bring about her demise, a benevolent voice echoing through the precincts of her spirit refused to accept the impending finality of her earthly existence. At the confluence of the negative whispers announcing that her days were rapidly winding down, a persistent voice affirmed that the end was not yet to be.

Energized by the resounding "Yes" of a new vitality cascading through the crevices of her spirit, the woman encountered a wellspring of courage with which to reset her spiritual compass in the direction of the "full life" whose only source is God. As such, she kept her spiritual frequencies attuned to echoes of grace that kept heralding good news that even though weeping may endure for the night, joy will certainly come in the morning.

Emboldened by a resurgence of spiritual defiance, the woman began paying closer attention to spellbinding reports of a Nazarene, named Jesus. The exhilarating news of miraculous healings that were accomplished by the itinerant rabbi from Nazareth, in Galilee, spread like wildfire throughout every village and hamlet within Israel. It had the effect of an exploding flare in her spirit, announcing that her dark midnight of suffering would soon vanish in the illumination of the approaching day of liberation.

Intent on capturing her rendezvous with destiny, the woman kept her ears attuned to the local grapevine. After discovering the location in her community where Jesus would be ministering, she strategically positioned herself at just the right place, in order to establish physical contact with him. With the imprimatur of pain etched on her face, she pressed herself forcefully into the pulsating throng surrounding the miracle-worker. When he arrived within arms length of where she was standing, she grabbed hold of the hem or tassel of his garment. At the very instant of her touch the bleeding stopped and she felt in her body that she was healed of the disease.

When the woman grabbed hold of the hem of his garment, Jesus felt virtue go out of him, signifying that her touch was more than just a casual gesture. The sensation our Lord experienced in his body indicated that her act was the consumation of a faith-transaction with heaven. By sheer strength of will, she engaged in a spiritual withdraw from heaven's bank of transformation and resurrection possibilities, laden with transcendent energy capable of re-creating and redirecting her destiny. For the first time in twelve years she experienced the rapture of being alive.

Being the earthly embodiment of resurrection possibilities, Jesus became aware that someone had taken a leap of faith into hitherto uncharted territory and the exercise of their faith was the catalyst that threw open the door to health and wholeness. Knowing what had recently transpired should never remain shrouded in secrecy, but showcased as an enduring testimonial to all humanity about the transformative power of faith, he turned to to his disciples and questioned: "Who touched me?" The puzzled disciples responded," "You see the crowd pressing around you and yet you say who touched me?"

Ignoring the response of his bewildered followers, Jesus peered intently into the vast gallery of faces to discover who was courageous enough to engage in such a tremendous leap of faith. The crescendo came when the woman acknowledged what had been done in her body. Unable to contain her gratitude any longer, she stepped forth with fear and trembling, prostrated herself before the Lord and disclosed the entire truth to him.

Demonstrating that personal faith would get from God that for which it believes, Jesus responded to the woman's confession saying, "Daughter thy faith has made thee whole. Go in peace and be healed of the plague."

When we dissect the amazing report, we are able to discern that the woman engaged in a series of purposeful activities that enabled her to attain her divine birthright of abundant life. The first such activity was that of turning her problem over to God.

After all the prominent medical specialists had exhausted their expertise and concluded that there was nothing more they could do to improve the patient's condition, she came to the realization that God alone was her Ability in a state of physical disability. Armed with the assurance that the government of her life was fully upon *His* shoulder, she offered up her problem to the Cosmic Healer.

When the bleeding woman began hearing recurring reports of Jesus and his amazing miracles, she became convinced by the envoys of hope that he was undeniably the Majesty of heaven enfleshed in the lowly garb of humanity and knew beyond the shadow of a doubt that he could cure her of her disease.

In her excitement to receive healing, she undoubtedly found it difficult to contain her enthusiasm and announced to family members and friends about her intentions to seek help from the Nazarene, only to be repeatedly reminded about the final and depressing prognosis of the many physicians who treated her condition in times past. The response of the individuals might have been reminiscent of the occasion when God directed His prophet, Ezekiel, to venture into a valley full of dry bones whose death scene reflected the spiritual devastation roiling the nation of Israel at that time. As he viewed the appalling desolation, God questioned him asking, "Son of man can these bones live?" (Ezekiel 37:3). In this instance, the question on everyone's lips was, "Can this broken wreck of humanity recapture a semblance of wholeness?"

In like manner as Ezekiel responded to God's question, the woman affirmed in her spirit, "O Lord God, Thou knowest." Motivated by a new-found exhilaration, she became intent on listening only to the silent witness that pulsated through the crevices of her spirit, providing her with assurance that God Almighty could accomplish what the most skilled medical practitioners of her day could not do, that being, heal her of the malignancy whose intractable grip had invaded and laid claim to her body for far too many years.

The Bible reminds us that the symbols of the cross and resurrection testify to the faith and hope that suffering can issue new life. And that we are afforded the sacred privilege and responsibility of becoming actively engaged in this paschal process by making a conscious choice as to *how* we will participate. By consciously choosing to endure suffering in such a way that we never become disconnected from, or stop loving the Life that is larger than our own circumstances, we are somehow able to turn suffering into the service of life and participate in the dying and resurrection of Jesus. By so doing, we develop the capacity to discern the presence of God in the here and now, suffering and overcoming through and with and in us.

The second kind of activity that the woman became engaged in was that of assuming a posture of receptivity. On those occasions when her stamina and hope were assailed by the sheer length of her painful journey and she experienced burnout from the long haul, she refused to shrink into an inner hell and instead opened up her spirit up the "gift of a higher life."

Honesty impels us to admit that it takes a tremendous amount of courage and energy to open ourselves up to the incursion of a higher life, especially in those instances when the cosmos becomes a dark, tangled place, devoid of meaning or purpose. But, even in the dark edges of human experiences when God's very presence seems profoundly hidden from us and we occasionally rail at Him for not appearing to be on top of things, we could still discover His immanent, tender presence, operative in our midst.

In the dark shadows of Gethsemane when Jesus became suffused with dread and anxiety concerning the circumstances surrounding his impending death, he cried out, "Father if it be possible, let this cup pass from me." Like many of us do when our lives become embroidered with adversity, he looked for an avenue of escape from his own pain predicament. But recognizing what offering up his life entailed for the human family, he declared, "Nevertheless, not my will, but thy will be done." Even though he experienced the tumultuous onslaught of despair, the cosmic proportions of his Father's unfolding redemptive plan rekindled within him the hope of resurrection and joy. This reality culminated in final words on the cross, indicating that his mission to earth was accomplished: "It is finished."

Jesus provided us with the example that we could likewise develop the capacity to envision suffering as a redemptive and transformative process, capable of ushering us across new thresholds into a realm of

transcendent possibilities, whereby we become empowered to "see" God with "new" eyes and to trust Him
with "new-found" faith. This however only becomes
possible when we expectedly choose to embrace words
that harness the confidence and promise that we can
hold on to hope, even when all rational ground for
holding on have been destroyed.

The third form of activity that the tenacious sister
engaged in was that of making a calculated decision of
positioning herself at a place where she would make
contact with Jesus. The "position" we assume in life is
indicative of our inner desire to receive impartation
from our heavenly Father. God demonstrated on
repeated occasions in the Bible that He will meet us in
any condition and situation, when we embark on a
spiritual journey in His direction.

When Mary Magdalene got wind of the fact that
Jesus was having dinner at the home of Simon the
Pharisee, she entered the Jewish religious leader's house
unannounced. In so many words, she crashed the man's
party. After gaining entrance to the residence, she broke
an alabaster of pure spikenard she had brought along
and positioned herself at the Master's feet. Weeping
uncontrollably, she wet his feet with tears and wiped
them with the hair of her head. When Simon observed
the unorthodox activity that was transpiring in his

house, he became indignant and reasoned within himself that if Jesus was truly a prophet, he would have known what sort of woman was touching him.

Discerning the thoughts of the self-righteous Pharisee, Jesus outlined a scenario involving a creditor and two individuals who were indebted to him. He indicated that one debtor owed the creditor five hundred pence and the other owed him fifty. When neither individual had the resources to repay their loan, the creditor demonstrated compassion by forgiving both of them. After completing the scenario, Jesus inquired of Simon as to which of the men would love the creditor most. Simon responded that in his estimation it would certainly be the one whom he forgave most. Jesus informed Simon that he was correct in his assumption.

Unexpectedly, Jesus notified Simon that he was a most ungracious host by pointing out that when he entered his residence he was provided no water to wash the dust off of his feet, which was customary for a host to do. He remarked that the woman seized the opportunity to wash his feet with her tears and delighted in wiping them with her hair. Knowing how fussy the vast majority of women are about hair, this was truly an act of love on her part. As a matter of fact, the Bible states that a woman's hair is her glory. As such, Mary utilized her glory to wipe the dust off of her Savior's feet!

Jesus went further and pointed out that upon his arrival his host neglected to welcome him with the customary kiss, while the party-crashing woman on the other hand had not ceased to kiss his feet. She was so enraptured by his divine personality and the opportunity to minister to him, that she was oblivious to the dust and grime covering his feet. In deep adoration she anointed his feet with precious ointment whose cost was equivalent to an entire year's salary. While she might have been a woman with a notorious reputation, she was certainly not cheap. Jesus was so impressed by her extravagant worship that he informed her that her *many* sins were forgiven, because she loved *much* and declared to the woman, "Thy sins be forgiven."

When the dinner guests overheard the seemingly blasphemous pronouncement that was uttered by Jesus, they questioned within themselves as to who he reckoned himself to be by believing that he had the authority to forgive sins.

It is evident that the position Mary assumed both physically and spiritually enabled her to become the recipient of salvation. In the first place, she did not allow any barrier to deny her access to the personality with the capacity to make her whole, even if it meant going against the grain of social protocol and crashing a private party. Her actions indicated that she was prepared to climb any mountain, swim any ocean or walk any distance, just as long as she eventually found herself in the presence of Jesus.

Secondly, like her sister with the issue of blood, Mary did the unthinkable by engaging in the desperate and dangerous act of touching a rabbi or holy man. This was unacceptable behavior for any woman to engage in. Jewish religious law prohibited unmarried couples of the opposite sex from mingling with each other. But what made matters worse in this particular instance was the fact that she was known by the residents of her local community as a woman with a tattered history. She had the unsavory reputation of being a harlot! A whore! And by touching a holy man she placed herself in the precarious position of being dragged to the edge of town and stoned to death for violating the ancient religious taboo. But rather than being preoccupied with the prohibitions of Jewish religious law, Jesus was more preoccupied with rekindling the smoldering embers of life that had been snuffed out on the woman's inside by a judgmental society bent on condemnation, rather than reconciliation. Recognizing that she had placed her life in jeopardy in order to become the recipient of new life, he provided her with much needed salvation.

The last, but certainly not the least kind of activity that the woman engaged in was that of seizing the opportunity to act on her situation in a timely manner. In other words, she refused to put off meeting Jesus for another day.

One of the greatest tragedies of life is the fact that far too many people put off doing tomorrow things that need to be accomplished today. By so doing, they allow unique opportunities to slip by and fail to take action to bring about transformation in their situation. The Bible tells us, "Now is the accepted time. Now is the day of salvation."

Another situation where someone became the recipient of salvation because of the position they assumed was Zaccheus (cf. Luke 19).

Zaccheus was a tax collector. Tax collectors in First Century Palestine were an unsavory bunch. They were considered by the Jewish religious authorities as social pariahs who were engaged in an occupation that excluded them from the "people of God," because they worked for Roman authorities in collecting taxes and other fees. They had cultivated a notorious reputation for defrauding people by demanding excessive taxes and pocketing the difference. Additionally, they had no scruples about engaging in mercenary activities by occasionally employing violence against innocent people, in order to achieve their sinister ends.

When Jesus came to Zaccheus' hometown of Jerico, the tax collector had a burning desire to have an encounter with the wandering rabbi. But there was one problem, Zaccheus was a man of little stature and would have found it impossible to have a face-to-face encounter with Jesus, because he would have been unable to see above the vast sea of curious heads that usually surrounded the Nazarene. While he might have been short, Zaccheus was extremely ingenious. He had to be, in order to be a successful thief. Employing shrewd instincts, he did what he had to do, in order to place himself in a position where he could establish contact with the miracle-worker from Nazareth, in Galilee. He hurriedly ran ahead of the pulsating crowd and climbed up into the branches of a sycamore tree.

When Jesus arrived at Zaccheus' location, he gazed intently up at the tree-dweller and instructed him to make haste and climb down from his high perch, because he was inviting himself to dinner at his house that very day. Scripture indicates that Zaccheus received the Master's word gladly and clamored down from the tree and escorted Jesus to his house.

Jesus is a discerner of thoughts and knew that while Zaccheus had become enriched by ill-gotten goods, he continued to be tormented by spiritual poverty that constantly gnawed at his inside. He lived under the daily illusion that riches would somehow fill the spiritual void in his life, only to become disappointed that the more riches he accumulated, the poorer he felt. However, when he learned that Jesus was coming to his hometown and knowing that he possessed words of life, Zaccheus decided that he would place himself in a position where he might find the answer to the spiritual poverty that robbed him of abundant life.

Scripture is silent on the intimate dinner conversation that transpired between Jesus and Zaccheus. However, the outcome is unmistakably clear. Zaccheus was so transformed by the words of the Master that the hard-hearted tax collector abandoned his wicked ways and confessed that he would give half of his goods to the poor and restore four times the amount of money to those from whom he defrauded in times past.

In each of the preceding scenarios where individuals had encounters with Jesus and became the recipient of salvation, we note the concrete particularity that runs like a thread through each story is the issue of *position*.

The French Catholic philosopher, Maurice Blondel (1861-1949), states that all our actions and choices determine who we are. All that we choose and do resonates with eternal implications of allegiance and identity; all our actions, therefore, are inherently religious. If we live our lives open to the "full life" whose only source is God, we are placing the will and "the action and being of God within ourselves." Ultimately, our lives are characterized by our choice to place ourselves in the position whereby we can open up ourselves to the gift of a "higher life," or, we could close up within ourselves, "pronounce [our] own condemnation."

The question confronting us every single moment of our existence is how do we refrain from pronouncing our own condemnation, when our world suddenly and unexpectedly tilts and breaks open and no amount of effort on our part seems capable of putting the shattered pieces back together again. At least not as it was? How do we continue to move forward towards health and wholeness, when we are perpetually confronted with the challenge of trying to find a footing in an unimaginably altered landscape? The answer to this pressing question is by continuing to love life wholeheartedly.

The Bible testifies that the greatest force in the universe is love. Writing to the church at Corinth, the apostle Paul, states that, "Love beareth all things, believeth all things, hopeth all things and *endureth* all things" (1 Corinthians 13:7). The words of the great apostle are much more than sentimental jargon, because love is a force field with the potential to impact our existence with a valence capable of transforming us in a most profound way.

The apostle John, states elsewhere, "In this is love, not that we love God, but that he loved us and sent his son to be the propitiation for our sins" (1 John 4:10). These powerful words continue to echo down through the corridors of time that the exalted Son of God pitched his tent in the midst of sinful humanity, in order that we might attain union with the One without boundaries.

In writing to the Church at Philippi, Paul shares John's sentiments by making what is undoubtedly one of the greatest declarations in the Bible regarding God's love for humanity:

[Christ Jesus], who though he was in the form of God, did not think being equal to God something to be grasped but emptied himself, taking the form of a slave,
born of human likeness.
And being found in human likeness,
He humbled himself,
Becoming obedient to death,
[even the death on a cross].
Therefore God hath highly exalted him,
and given him a name above every other name,
that at the name of Jesus every knee should bend,
[in heaven and on earth and under the earth],

and every tongue confess that Jesus Christ is Lord,
to the glory of God, the Father.

(Philippians 2:7-11).

It is refreshing to know that God is no casual observer in the drama of human suffering. He did not
acquire a casual academic acquaintance with the human
condition by standing on the sidelines to experience it
vicariously. Instead, he became robed in sinful flesh, in
order that He might actively participate in the stream of
humanity. Therefore, when we hurt, God hurts. Only
one who joins us in weeping can assure us that when
storms blow into our lives, we can rest assured that love
never ends.

The reigning assumption of our spirit that keeps us
grounded in our heavenly Father's love is the fact that
in Christ *we are more than conquerors.* Because of the
exalted position our Lord assumed at the right hand of
the Father after his resurrection and ascension back to
heaven, his position as Advocate, Intercessor and
Mediator, on our behalf, places the entire universe
under *his* authority, including our particular circumstances. The Bible declares that our Lord was given *all*
power in heaven and earth. And he imparts supernatural power to liberate us from the powers of darkness
that conspire to impede our access to abundant life. In
this vein, we need never succumb to disillusionment,

but instead, hold on to *his* hem from which streams of life ensue and rest assured that we are likewise being held by a grace that is larger than anything that might confront us on this side of glory.

Chapter Two

An Oil Well in an Oil Jar
(2 Kings 4:1-7)

෴

In those instances when we find it difficult to arrive at a final conclusion on some matter based entirely on what is observed by the naked eye, we are inclined to say that something "more than meets the eye." In other words, the situation is far more complex than it appears at first glance and could be likened to an iceberg whose tip is visible above the surface of the water, while seventy to ninety per cent of the object's mass remains submerged beneath the waterline.

Like the greater mass of the iceberg lying concealed beneath the surface of the water, God's mysteries and wonders invariably remain inaccessible at the boundaries of our rationalistic capabilities. In our quest to plumb the deep mysteries of life, we are frequently brought to the place where we come to realize that revelation of divine truth demands a heightened state of spiritual acuity and devotional well-being, in order that the Holy Spirit might transport us beyond the borders of our rationalistic assumptions to a heightened sense of wonder, awe and reverence for our Creator and His amazing possibilities. The narrative of Second Kings, Chapter Four, serves such a purpose. It is as an enduring testimonial, pointing to a higher understanding of the Christian faith and challenges us to step beyond our conditioned presuppositions, in order to see the activity of God in the world in a new light. By so doing, we open ourselves up to an expanded worldview — the not-yet revealed world that God is prepared to offer us.

The ancient narrative recounts the dilemma of a poor widow who was literally stopped in her tracks by adversity. However, adversity did not end up becoming her final destination in life, because she came to the realization that God's providential care encompasses even the worst scenarios life has to offer.

Before the woman's husband died, he was one of the sons of the prophets and died leaving her with the burden of caring for two sons. Like most wives of prophets who survived their husbands in those days, she expectedly encountered hard times that rendered her broke and penniless. In an effort to survive the hard stretch of road on which she suddenly found herself, she did what most women in her situation did when confronted by hardship. She secured the services of a creditor who provided her with a loan that enabled her family to survive the lean times. But lacking any concrete source of income with which to honor the stipulated terms of repayment, she eventually defaulted on the loan. Unconcerned about the woman's predicament, the creditor demanded immediate repayment by invoking an ancient Jewish law that would enable him to recoup his financial outlay.

Under Mosaic Law, creditors were empowered to claim the person and children of any debtor who lacked the wherewithal to repay loans. Such individuals were legally obligated to serve the creditor until the arrival of the Year of Jubilee, which occurred every 50th year in Israel (Leviticus 25). Three essential characteristics define this year. The first stipulation indicated that any Israelite who was currently in bondage to any of their countrymen would be set free. The law also decreed that the price of slaves would vary according to the proximity of Jubilee Year.

The second stipulation demanded that ancestral possessions be returned to those who had been compelled to sell them when they became ensnared by poverty. This of course excluded the possibility of selling a piece of land permanently.

The third feature of the of the law required that throughout the Year of Jubilee the land would remain fallow, in order that nutrient-depleted soil might replenish itself.

Under the first article of the ancient code, the widow's creditor was legally empowered to lay claim to her two boys. The siblings were then subjected to be pressed into service by the creditor, until such time as they worked off the outstanding balance of their mother's loan obligation or the Day of Jubilee arrived.

There is no greater pain a mother could experience comparable to that of losing the fruit of her womb. It is a request too great to be borne. But in this particular scenario, life was being extremely cruel by subjecting the widow to a double blow — the recent loss of her husband and the impending seizure of two sons. Like a drowning swimmer caught up in the swirling crosscurrents of her tumultuous ordeal, the woman was pushed to the brink of despair — to a place where she became dispirited by the disturbing dilemma. Visualizing no possible avenue of escape from the pain-drenched predicament, she realized the necessity of consulting Elisha who was the current head of the school of prophets in Israel.

After encountering the man of God, the woman tearfully unburdened herself by disclosing that the creditor had come to take her sons away to press them into service as bondsmen, because she defaulted on the loan that was incurred subsequent to the death of her husband. After listening to the heart-rending lament emanating from the sorrowful mass of humanity standing before him, Elisha questioned, "What shall I do for you?" In light of existing circumstances this seemed to be an unusual question to ask a bereaved widow who recently experienced the loss of her beloved husband and whose babies were about to be snatched from her bosom by an unsympathetic creditor. Reflecting on the information she had provided thus far, she recalled stating that her husband — Elisha's servant was dead. But the prophet should have been aware of this fact already, since he was the dead man's superior. She also recalled stating that the creditor was poised to legally remove both sons from the family home. In lieu of this reality, why would anyone in his or her right mind question, "What shall I do for you?" She assumed that seeking the prophet out and presenting her case to him was a declaration that she was in dire straits — so she thought.

The look of confusion on the woman's face apparently signaled to Elisha that his line of questioning was somewhat unnerving and that she was in desperate need of help, not silly and irritating questions. Elisha undoubtedly sensed that the trauma ensuing from the death of the woman's husband was now being compounded by the legal stipulation that she surrender her boys to servitude and responded to her lament with the question: "Tell me, what do you have in your house?"

The widow was yet again confused by Elisha's strange line of questioning and concluded that he was obviously inquiring about some commodity with a significant economic value attached to it. She however reckoned that had this been the case she would have disposed of the item a long time ago, in order to secure resources that would have enabled her to liquidate her financial obligation to the creditor. She reasoned that had this transpired already there would have been no need to seek the prophet out and be subjected to a disturbing barrage of questioning.

Being careful not to scuttle her chances of receiving any relief that might be forthcoming from Elisha, the widow refrained from responding to the old man's questions in a politically incorrect manner. She reflected on the strange question, but after conducting a mental inventory of her household possessions, the only item her mind eventually settled on was an inconsequential jar of oil sitting on a shelf. She informed Elisha that there was nothing of significant economic value in her house except a dusty little jar of oil.

Elisha instructed the woman to take her sons throughout the neighborhood and borrow every available empty vessel they could lay their hands on. After completing the assignment, they were to return home, shut themselves behind closed doors and commence pouring oil from the little jar into each vessel, until every single vessel was full.

The widow apparently had no difficulty responding to the strange request, because her family members were already familiar with the miracle-working ability of the ancient prophet. As such, they had high expectations for a miracle of their own. With their lives hanging in limbo, they refrained from questioning the rationale of the strange directive and obediently complied with the unusual request.

After receiving their assignment, the threesome feverishly crisscrossed every highway and byway like busy worker bees, knocking energetically on doors and imploring neighbors to loan them any empty vessel they possibly could. They worked non-stop until every available lending source had been exhausted.

After completing the first phase of the assignment, the angst-ridden mother and her two sons retreated back to the confines of the family home, shut themselves behind closed doors and began pouring oil from the dusty little jar into borrowed containers. For untold hours they were enraptured by a divine bliss brought about by the birthing of a miracle under their roof as oil flowed from a mysterious source within the little jar, finally stopping when there were no other vessels left to fill.

Elated over her new-found wealth, the widow hurried back to Elisha and provided him with a detailed report of the qualitative change brought about on account of her obedience to his directive. She was "off the hook," as it pertained to her indebtedness and the broad smile on her face said it all. In no way revealing that he expected an alternative outcome, Elisha instructed the elated mother to sell her bounty and use the funds to settle scores with her creditor. He further advised her that after selling all that she could, she and her sons could live off of the resources ensuing from the sale of whatever oil they had remaining.

Like the woman with the issue of blood, the widow responded to adversity by first turning to the *Source* that would ultimately transform her situation. While Elisha himself was not the Source of transformation, he was a power of attorney on earth of the Source — a conduit to the Source. As such, he had access to the divine storehouse and demonstrated through his ministry that when we confront impoverishment in the earthly economy, there is never a famine in the divine economy.

David, the sweet Psalmist of Israel declared: "I will look to the hills from which cometh my help…" (Psalm 121:1). The spiritual implication or reference to hills is extremely significant. In Biblical parlance hills denote height or *high* places. Not necessarily in terms of physical, but spiritual dimensions. It really signifies the need to deploy our faith to the farthest reaches of the heavens, in order that we might enter the stream of endless possibilities emanating from the throne of Almighty God. Because the hopes and aspirations of many individuals are not anchored in Almighty God and the stream of infinite possibilities that accrue to us when we entrust our circumstances to Him, some folks make the unfortunate decision of turning to, or looking in *low* places for consolation. They become involved in pursuits that are ultimately incapable of bringing about meaningful changes in their situation. We know this to be true, because we are daily bombarded in the media by propaganda that tantalizes the viewing audience with vulgar proliferations of psychic hotlines. Such enticements is the doorway to a prison house where desperate, weak-minded individuals become intoxicated and entrapped with the concoctions of electronic quacks, who further exacerbate the problems of gullible victims, rendering them worse off than before.

The widow came to the end of a long tunnel of tragedy and tribulation when she turned to God. The truth of the matter is that we will always experience transformation in our life situation when we make the conscious decision of turning to God. So, even though we might at times be rendered powerless to change the way our world spins, it is entirely within our power to change the direction we are facing — regardless of the way this unwilling world may turn. The decision to look to the Source from which our help comes, will change the world for us, because it changes our relationship with the world. It changes our relationship with the world, because by making the conscious decision to look to the Source of all help, our circumstances will no longer be governed by external happenings. But by that One who reigns supreme over every happening.

Chapter Three

Visualize What Else
(2 Kings 6:8-23)

⌘

Jesus had it right! He always visualized the world as an ongoing expression of the Spirit. From his unique perspective, creation was gracious and loving and ultimately revealed the glory of God. As far as Jesus was concerned, life was in and of itself a sacred benediction.

By drawing on images from nature, Jesus had the uncanny ability of challenging his contemporaries to utilize spiritual eyes, rather than physical eyes, as a prism through which they might view life. He declared on one occasion, "Look at the birds of the air..." and "Consider the lilies..." (Matthew 6:25, 28). In other words, he challenged humankind to change the way we see the world and be responsive to the presence or activity of the divine that is operative in our midst. This admonition continues to be one of the biggest challenges confronting humanity today. The truth of the matter is those individuals from all walks of life who develop the capacity to visualize the world as dynamic and pulsing with divine energy, rather than inanimate and impersonal are inevitably the ones who develop the capacity to push the ceiling of possibility to a higher level. Rather than visualizing "what is," they become empowered to visualize "what else."

Scripture reveals that if we rely on our deepest faith in times of crisis and pray for enlightenment to visualize alternative realities when we find ourselves hemmed in by destruction, the Spirit breathing through us can create fresh possibilities that announce the new life of the Resurrection. This reality is corroborated in an ancient narrative nestled in the Old Testament Book of Second Kings, Chapter Six and verses eight to eighteen.

The report states that the king of Syria devised plans to wage war against Israel. After consulting with advisers, he decided that he would establish camp at a strategic location that would afford him the opportunity to engage in a preemptory attack against Israel. In so many words, it was an ambush! After being informed by the Spirit as to the intent of the king of Syria, Elisha briefed the king of Israel concerning his adversary's war plans. When the king of Syria realized that the king of Israel was somehow being informed of his motives, he became irate and suspected that there was a traitor in his midst who was leaking confidential information to the Israelite king.

The king of Syria initiated an investigation to flush out the informer he suspected of being in his camp. However, one of the king's men spoke up and informed him that there was no informer in his camp. Instead, he disclosed that it was the prophet Elisha who was providing information to the king of Israel concerning even the things that he discussed in the privacy of his bedchamber. The king of Syria became furious when he received the unsettling news and sent spies to apprehend Elisha after it was reported that he was in Dothan, a distance of about fourteen miles north of Samaria.

The king of Syria deployed horses, chariots and a great army under the cover of darkness and surrounded the city of Dothan. In the morning when the servant of Elisha awoke and saw the mighty Syrian Army surrounding the city, he panicked and ran to Elisha lamenting, "Alas my master! What shall we do?" Elisha responded to his servant telling him, "Fear not: for they that be with us are more than they that be with them." Elisha then prayed saying, "Lord, I pray thee, open his eyes that he might see." The Lord responded to Elisha's prayer by opening the eyes of the young man and he suddenly saw that the mountains were full of horses and chariots (2 Kings 6:17). This is an important revelation in Scripture regarding men on earth receiving insight into the invisible world of spirit beings, by revealing that the mountain were filled with spirit chariots and horses that came for Elisha and his servant. There were innumerable chariots and horses, which could not be perceived by the natural eye, except through divine adjustment.

When the Syrian Army approached the wall of the city and made the demand that Elisha be surrendered to them, Elisha was already prepared for their appearance and prayed that God would smite the Syrian soldiers with blindness. The Lord answered and did as His servant requested. The prophet then led the entire Syrian Army to the City of Samaria, suggesting that the man they wanted was at that location. This was more truth than it appears on the surface, since it was really the king of Israel that they were seeking, not Elisha. As such, Elisha led them to the very man against whom they were desirous of making war. When the Syrian Army was safe in the hands of the King of Israel, Elisha prayed for God to open their eyes and when He did, they looked upon the two men they wanted — the king of Israel and the man who was revealing their most intimate secrets. The king of Israel was inclined to decimate the Syrian Army. They were however saved by Elisha who requested that they be fed and released back to their master, the king of Syria. When the Syrian troops had eaten to their heart's content, they were afforded the opportunity to return to their own country. This compassionate gesture was enough to prove to them that Israel had made no plans to harm the Syrian people. The goodness on the part of Israel made the Syrian Army ashamed of their plans for war. As such, they came no more into the land of Israel for some time.

When we take the time to really reflect on this insightful narrative, we are able to capture a sense of awe that emerges in the report — that being, we are forever being cradled by a hope powerful enough to hold life in its fragility. The fact that we are forever being cradled by divine hope, challenges us to push the boundaries of self and the world from that what is, to what it could be. This must have been the illumination that influenced the writer Phillip Brooks to declare, "Dreadful will be the day when the world becomes contented, when one universal satisfaction spreads itself over the world. Sad will be the day for every man when he becomes absolutely contented with the life that he is living, with the thoughts that he is thinking, with the deeds that he is doing, where there is not forever beating at the doors of his soul some great desire to do something larger which he knows that he was made to do because he is a child of God"

One person, who knew beyond the shadow of a doubt that he possessed the inherent capacity to accomplish an astounding feat, because he cultivated the insight to visualize an alternate reality other than the status quo, was Sir Roger Bannister.

Roger Bannister was born in Harrow, Middlesex, England, in 1929. He first enjoyed success as an athlete in his early teens, winning several foot races. But it was the combining of his later scientific knowledge with his athletic ability that would eventually enable him to become enshrined in the pantheon of legends.

In 1946, Bannister enrolled in Oxford University where he pursued studies in the field of medicine. He later completed his medical training at St. Mary's Hospital in London and devoted all of his spare time to track and field athletics and became an accomplished middle distance runner. The burning fascination for middle distance men at that time was the breaking of the four-minute barrier, which many believed was an impossible feat for a human being. It is rumored that quite a few of Bannister's colleagues in the medical profession advised him that if he ever attempted such a feat his heart would literally jump right out of his body. However, this sort of advice did not deter Bannister from persevering towards his objective. He believed that the goal of running a mile in under four minutes was an attainable goal and utilized his knowledge as a physician to provide him with as much help as possible in achieving his objective. As such, he painstakingly researched mechanical aspects of running and developed scientific training methods to assist him in his quest to run a sub four-minute mile.

By the time 1954 had come around, Bannister was vying with another great runner to become the first human to break the four-minute barrier — John Landy of Australia. Both men had demonstrated the potential to break the barrier in previous races, but the magic figure continued to be an elusive target.

It was at Iffley Road, Oxford, on May 6, 1954, that Roger Banister finally achieved his life's dream. He was aided and abetted by two pacesetters, Chris Brasher and Chris Chatway. He had done quite a bit of preparation at Paddington Green during the previous week for the race, where he was compelled to compete with high winds. The weather at Iffley Road on race day was a bit unusual as well — a 15 mph crosswind with gusts up to 25 mph Banister was so disillusioned by the uncooperative weather conditions that he nearly called the attempt off.

When the starter's pistol went off, Chris Brasher immediately took the lead as the first pacesetter. Bannister slotted in right behind him, with Chatway following in third place. When Brasher showed signs of tiring, Bannister gave the signal for Chatway to take over as pacesetter. At the sound of the bell for the last lap it was he, Chatway, who was in the lead with a time of just over three minutes. With just over two hundred yards from the finish line, Roger Bannister became infused with a herculean surge of energy and bolted like a rocket into the lead, crossing the finish line in a time of three minutes fifty-nine point four seconds. His name had not only been indelibly inscribed in the record books, but in sporting folklore as well.

After Bannister broke the four minute barrier, it was again broken two months later by his rival Landy, indicating that the previous time was as much a psychological as well as a physical barrier.

In his later years Dr. Roger Bannister, M.D., devoted his efforts to the practice of medicine. He was knighted by the Queen of England in 1975 and was appointed Master of Pembroke College, Oxford, from 1985-1993. But despite his stellar achievements in the fields of medicine and education, Sir Roger Bannister, M.D., will forever be remembered at the man who ran the miracle mile. By sheer strength of will, he was determined to visualize "what else," instead of "what is."

Roger Bannister's accomplishment proved to be such an extraordinary feat that it literally reverberated across the entire planet, in like manner as the subsequent occasion when humans first set foot on the surface of the moon. This later feat was also accomplished because the American president, John F. Kennedy, was able to visualize horizons where no other human had ventured before.

John Fitzgerald Kennedy (1917-1963) was the youthful 35th president of the United States of America. He was born in Brookline, Massachusetts and was the son of Joseph Kennedy, former U.S. Ambassador to Britain. Kennedy studied at Harvard University and later served as a P.T. boat commander during World War II. His book *Profiles in Courage* (1956), won a Pulitzer Prize. He was elected Democratic Representative (1947) and Senator (1952) for Massachusetts. Not only is he recognized as one of the outstanding personalities of history, he also cultivated the insight to visualize an alternate reality to the one currently in existence.

Up to that point in history, Kennedy was the second youngest president to occupy the White House (Theodore Roosevelt was the youngest). His quest to assume what many regard as the most powerful political office on the planet was not greeted with unbridled enthusiasm, because he lacked the support of several influential people within the Democratic Party. Confronted with lukewarm and at times no support from powerful individuals within the party hierarchy, there were additionally those who were prejudiced against the young Irishman, because of his Catholic heritage. Harry Truman (1884-1972), the 33rd president of the United States of America who was alive at the time and himself an arbiter of power with the Democratic Party, questioned Kennedy's readiness for the world stage at his youthful age of forty-three. Eleanor Roosevelt, wife of Franklin D. Roosevelt, the 32nd president of the United States of America, pledged her political capital to the camp of Kennedy's rival in the Democratic Party who was also campaigning to occupy the Oval Office. Despite the chilly rebuff from the shakers and movers within the ranks of his own political party, John F. Kennedy attained his dream of being elected president of the United States of America in 1960.

In a radio and television report to the American people on July 25, 1961, the youthful president delivered a landmark address concerning America's continued exploration of space. He declared during the address, "First I believe that this nation should commit itself to achieving the goal, before this decade is out, of landing a man safely on the moon and returning him to earth. No single space project in this period will be more impressive to mankind or important for the long-range exploration of space. And none will be more difficult or expensive to accomplish."

Many skeptics listening to President Kennedy's proclamation might have assumed that he was indulging in pipe dreams. But, John F. Kennedy was determined to think big. Unfortunately, he was felled by an assassin's bullet on November 22, 1963, in Dallas, Texas, denying him the opportunity of seeing his space dream become a reality.

In July 1969, Buzz Aldrin, Neil Armstrong and Michael Collins, set out on a successful Moon-Landing expedition and on July 20, 1969, Armstrong and Aldrin became the first men to set foot on the lunar surface. After the spectacular conquering of the alien planet, the entire Apollo 11 crew accomplished a successful return to earth. Because John F. Kennedy was prepared to visualize what others might have thought to be an outlandish — nay an impossible feat, America's Space Program reached a new milestone in history. Kennedy visualized "what else," instead of "what is."

The Bible teaches us to walk by faith and not solely by eyesight. In other words, we are exhorted to live by faith and not by emotional appetizers or intellectual delights. The Greeks referred to faith as divine madness, because it does not align with rationalistic assumptions of human thinking. And it cannot be explained within the framework of scientific calibration. Faith is the art of achieving in act what one has visualized in insight. This is certainly true of the life situation of the bumble bee.

It is claimed that in accordance with the laws of aerodynamics the bumble bee is not supposed to fly. Scientists have discovered that the wings of the insect are much too fragile to produce lift capability for the massive body to which they are attached. However, somewhere down the line someone forgot to inform the bumble bee about this fact. God must have given the bumble bee a flight assignment at creation and never sat down to discuss whether or not the specifications He created for its body were in perfect alignment with the laws of physics. By the same token, the bumble bee did not sit around and lament about his puny wings, nor question God about the plausibility of his flight assignment. Despite his obvious limitations, he took God at His word that he could fly and simply took off flying. The rest is history.

Like the bumble bee, we could likewise embark on flights into uncharted territory when we take God at his word. Despite the seeming limitations we might be confronted with, trusting in His word will usher us to new horizons. Every moment of every hour of every day, Jesus beckons us to visualize new realties. He states, "Behold! I make all things new" (Revelation 21:5) and reminds us, "Do not fear, only believe" (Mark 5:36b). The eternal Son of God pitched his tent in the midst of humanity and for thirty-three years walked through our ordinary hours and locations to gather them up and sanctify them as he passed. As such, he is intimately acquainted with the woof and warp of human life. The Bible states that the Word became flesh and embarked on a faith journey for his heavenly Father, in order to make atonement for the human family. Because he became engaged in the same thick tangle of dailiness as the rest of us, so can we. Let us join our Lord in a pilgrimage to embrace his "new thing," and visualize "what else"

Chapter Four

Waiting till My Change Comes
(Job 14:14b)

ঌ৵৶

The manner in which we respond to the challenges of life ultimately consists of a choice, whether conscious, or unconscious. Ultimately, it is not what life throws at us, but the way we choose to respond to what is thrown at us, determines our well-being.

The Old Testament story of Job is familiar to the vast majority of us and the book is named after its main character, Job, who possessed the amazing capacity to endure suffering and still maintain allegiance to his Creator.

Scripture indicates that Job hailed from the land of Uz, located somewhere near the borders of the desert that separates the eastern and western arms of the

Fertile Crescent (an area reaching NW from the Persian Gulf through Mesopotamia, then west to the north of Syria, then SW through Palestine). He was a perfect and upright man who feared God and hated evil and his enormous assets made him the wealthiest man in the entire east. His substance consisted of seven thousand sheep, three thousand camels, five hundred yoke of oxen and five hundred she asses. He was also the father of seven sons and three daughters.

Job had no inkling that the turmoil he would encounter ensued from the fact that God decided to showcase him as a pillar of uprightness. The Biblical narrative indicates that on a certain day when angels in heaven came to present themselves before Jehovah, Satan came also among them. The Lord questioned Satan, "When comest thou?" and he answered, "From going to and fro in the earth, and from walking up and down in it." The Lord said to Satan, "Hast thou considered my servant Job, that there is none like him in the earth, a perfect an upright man, one that feareth God and escheweth evil." Satan responded telling God that the only reason Job feared Him, was the fact that He had established a hedge about him and his family and blessed the work of his hands, thereby causing his substance to increase. He suggested however, that if God were to withdraw His protection and bring destruction to Job's property, he would certainly curse him to His face.

After listening to Satan's response, God granted him limited permission to test His servant Job. He withheld protection from Job and turned him over to the adversary for him to begin his unsavory experiment on him. This action on the part of God opened to floodgates of adversity into Job's life (Job 1:7-12).

The first episode of adversity occurred on a day when Job's sons and daughters were making merry at a banquet at his eldest son's house. He received a report indicating that the oxen were plowing in the field with the asses feeding beside them, when the Sabeans (Arab Bedouins) attacked and killed all of his servants, except the one who escaped to present him with the report. After killing the servants, the attackers carted off the animals.

While the first servant was still presenting Job with a report of the Sabean attack, another servant came along and informed him than lightning fell from heaven and consumed all 7,000 of his sheep and the servants that were tending them.

Before the second report of adversity could sink in, Job received a third report from another servant who escaped calamity to inform him that three bands of Chaldeans fell upon his servants who were caring for his 3,000 camels, killed them all and carted off the animals.

The destruction of Job's property was undoubtedly a tremendous blow to him, but little did he realize that his ordeal was far from being over. While he was receiving the report of the most recent calamity, another servant came along and informed him that his sons and daughters were eating and drinking at his eldest son's house and a great wind — possibly a desert whirlwind, blew out of the wilderness and smote the house and it collapsed on his children who were inside and killed them all. Only the servant who presented him with the report survived to tell what happened.

After receiving the chilling report concerning the death of his beloved children, Job arose, rent his clothes, shaved his head and fell on the ground and worshipped God. He lamented: "Naked came I out of my mother's womb, and naked shall I return thither: the Lord gave, and the Lord hath taken away; blessed be the name of the Lord."

Job had the amazing insight to recognize that he could not resist the sovereignty of God. Not only did he maintain his spiritual composure, but even in the teeth of adversity he found occasion for praise. It is quite possible that in measuring the greatness of his loss, he took stock of the abundance, which had all the while been entrusted, to his stewardship. But more importantly, the hour of desolation was a pivotal moment of truth for him. At a time when he was stripped naked of all his material possessions, he was unusually sensible to God's confronting presence and deep was suddenly constrained to cry out unto deep. Job's adoring heart undoubtedly responded in the presence of God with doxology: "Whom have I in heaven but thee? And there is none upon earth that I desire beside thee" (Psalm 73:25). Satan had prophesied that if Job were suddenly bereft of all of his earthly possessions, he would curse God (Job 1:11). But instead, Job blessed his Savior.

On a subsequent occasion Satan presented himself before God and yet again God boasted to him about His servant Job and how he maintained steadfast in faith, despite the adversity to which he had been subjected. Satan responded telling God, "Skin for skin, yea, all that a man hath he will give for his life. But put forth thine hand now and touch his bone and flesh and he will curse thee to thy face" (Job 2:4-5).

Satan's response insinuated that even Job's doxology, born in anguish of bereavement, was nothing more than the calculated response of a shrewd bargainer. Even though he was disappointed that God did not allow him to keep any of his possession, Job concealed his bitterness over his losses out of profane concern for

67

his physical well-being, thus the statement: "All that a man hath he will give for his life." The implication of this remark is that by doxology Job feigned love for God as the exorbitant, but necessary fee for health insurance. By imploring God to allow him to "Touch his bone and his flesh," Satan, implies that there will be no profit left in "the religious deal" and Job will resort to profanity and curse God to His face. So, once again, God allows the mystery of affliction to engulf His servant by allowing Satan to smite him with boils from the crown of his head to the soles of his feet.

There is no unanimous medical opinion concerning Job's affliction, but the general consensus of that day was the fact that it was an incurable disease. His entire body was smitten with loathsome and painful symptoms that included inflamed eruptions accompanied by intense itching (Job 2:7-8), maggots in ulcers (Job 7:5), erosion of the bones (Job 30:17), blackening and falling off of the skin (Job 30:30), and terrifying nightmares (Job 7:14). Even though Satan was obliged to spare his life, Job undoubtedly believed that death was imminent. The former prince of eastern patriarchs, revered above all of his brethren as the salt of the earth, is suddenly reduced to the status of an outcast who is unceremoniously driven from society and is now dwelling in utter desolation on what was probably the town dunghill.

Job's position on the garbage heap mirrors the trajectory of his life situation, as he plummets from the pinnacle of prosperity into abject poverty. As he sat scraping his oozing sores with pieces of broken pottery, his wife came along and suggested that he curse God and die, in order to be taken out of his misery. The temptation of Job's wife is remarkably similar to the temptation of Adam by Eve (Genesis 3). Each woman succumbed to adversary and became the instrument for the undoing of her husband. Satan cunningly spared the life of Job's wife for later use in the assault on his soul. Her blasphemous prophesy was exactly what Satan had prophesied of Job, but her evil counsel brought this phase of Job's torment to its fiercest pitch, indicating that she was one of the "foolish women." He did not necessarily call his wife a fool, but indicated that she spoke out of desperation. The behavior of Job's wife stands in sharp relief to his genuine piety, as he practices restraint in laying any blame at the doorstep of his Creator.

During an interval in which Job's spirit is stretched taut by the unrelenting torment to which his body is subjected by the ravages of the foul disease which disfigured him beyond recognition, three of his best friends showed up — Eliphaz the Tenamite, Bildad the Shuhite and Zophar the Naamathite. His cherished companions and counselors of "the greatest of all the men of the east" must have been princes of their respective people and sages of renown. Tenam in Edom was proverbial for wisdom (Jeremiah 49:7). The Shuhite tribe (cf. Genesis 25:2-6) and Naamah, were doubtlessly located in the east country, land of wise men (cf. 1 Kings 4:30).

Although Job's friends were aware of his calamity, they were unprepared for what they would encounter. They were so utterly devastated by his emaciated condition that their weeklong silence was like mourning for the dead (cf. Genesis 50:10; 1 Samuel 31:13). However, the moratorium of silence on the part of Job's three friends did not last forever. They soon began to accuse him of having done something extremely bad, in order to be reaping the kind of dividends he was. This was another phase of aggravation and spiritual torment on the part of Satan who subtly employed Job's well-intentioned comforters as his unwitting accomplices.

Eliphaz who was apparently the eldest of Job's friends (cf. Job 15:10) and thus the possessor of the most seasoned wisdom was accorded the dignity to first address Job and sets the direction by presenting his theory of sin and suffering by applying it to Job's situation. The fundamental, but false assumption of Eliphaz is that righteousness ultimately brings prosperity and wickedness adversity. He indicated that there is a direct correlation between sin and suffering and first addresses himself to Job's despondency (Job 4:2-11), then to his impatience (Job 4:12:-5:7) and finally counsels his friend to repent (Job 5:8-27).

Eliphaz accepted the view of the Eastern sages that extreme calamity follows acts of wickedness and believes that even though the righteous are subjected to seasons of suffering, they are not entirely cut off by God. From such observations Eliphaz deduces his law of sin and suffering and assumes that it must uniformly and universally govern human history. Unfortunately, Eliphaz's method of constructing the doctrine of providence is unreliable, in lieu of the fact that true theology rests on the authority of divine revelation and not limited human observation and fallible speculation.

Job eventually responds to his friend Eliphaz (Job 6:1-7:21) and knew that his extraordinary suffering could not be accounted for on the grounds of extraordinary sins. In responding, the patriarch does not engage in a theological discussion about God's justice, but vents against his inner ferment and the consequence about his sense of estrangement from God who afflicted him. This was apparently the undercurrent of Job's complain about his situation and Eliphaz's remarks appeared to aggravate it. He laments: "My brethren have dealt deceitfully as a brook and as the streams of brooks they pass away" (Job 6:15). He never expected any special favors, only the natural consolation one would come to expect from close friends. Yet, he was bitterly disappointed in his three "comforters" and viewed them as a thirsty desert caravan when it reaches the eagerly anticipated brook — sometimes a rushing, dark torrent — and finds not even a trickle among the rocks.

Bildad was the next person to address Job and proved to be just as insensitive as Eliphaz concerning his friend's predicament. He spurned Job's complaint about his condition, ignored the perceived unsympathetic approach of his friends and proceeds to provide Job with more of Eliphaz's counsel, all in the name of divine justice and venerable tradition. As it pertained to the defense of his innocence, Bildad questions Job, "How long wilt thou speak these things? And how long shall the words of thy mouth be a strong wind" (Job 8:2).

Behind Bildad's rhetorical question lay the judgment that Job was reaping a harvest of sin. In response to his condition Job contemplated his destiny more from the metaphysical perspective of divine transcendence and human finitude. But by focusing on the judicial aspect, the comforters only succeeded in intensifying their friend's aggravation. Job's theodicy was as inadequate as theirs and reason should have told him that God was deeply displeased with him. But his conscience refused to acknowledge transgression commensurate with his suffering. Bildad implored Job, "If thou wouldest seek unto God betimes, and make thy supplication to the Almighty. If thou were pure and upright; surely now he would awake for thee, and make the habitation of the righteousness prosperous" (Job 8:5-6). The exhortation is an astonishingly heartless, but consistent application of Bildad's thesis. Though the form is conditional, the intent is declarative. Since Job's afflictions did not yet prove fatal, as his children did, he may entertain hope that he is not, like them, reprobate and that his repentance will be followed by a restoration of blessings surpassing his former prosperity.

Job responded to Bildad with a sarcastic endorsement of his friend's opening (and fundamental) theme, "I know it is so of a truth; but how should a man be just with God? If he will contend with him, he cannot answer him one of a thousand. He is wise in heart and mighty in strength: who hath hardened himself against him and hath prospered" (Job 9:2-3). Job's statement did not indicate that man, being a fallen mortal, cannot stand in his own integrity before God. What he really indicated was that no matter what the righteousness of a man's cause might be, he is too puny and ignorant to successfully defend it in court before the overwhelming wisdom and power of God. The very thought of God's transcendence led Job to question why God should bother to afflict a frail man. Now the same thought provokes the question, why should a frail man bother to contend against God? This question expresses Job's loss of the sense of God's loving kindness. The Almighty appears to confront him like a giant adversity and as time evolves the sufferer bewails his sorrow, continuing to interpret them as tokens of divine condemnation. The urge to suppress his longing for a day in the divine court becomes overwhelming, though he has no hope of being granted such a privilege. Hence, he continued to reason earnestly with the strange God, the phantom creation of his frenzied doubt.

After a while Job's third friend, Zophar, addresses him and in like manner as Eliphaz and Bildad before him, intensely protested any innocence on the part of Job. Zophar bluntly condemns Job's alleged iniquity stating, "Should not the multitude of words be answered? And should a man full of talk be justified? Should thy lies make men hold their peace? And when thou mockest, shall no man make thee ashamed? For thou hast said, "My doctrine is pure, and I am clean in thine eyes. But oh that God would speak and open his lips against thee; And that he would shew thee the secrets of wisdom, that they are double to that which is! Know therefore that God exacteth of thee less thine thy iniquity deserveth" (Job 11:2-6).

Job insisted all along that God had afflicted him even though he was righteous (Job 11:4; 9:21; 10:7). That, Zophar points out contradicted traditional theory, is irreligious and cannot be allowed to stand as the last word. Zophar's distaste for Job's stance is evidenced by the fact that he dispensed with the customary courtesies and distaste and accusation merges with apology, "Oh that God would speak and open his lips against thee." Job seems irrepressible in controversy with his three best friends. But if he were granted the very thing he himself longs for, an open debate with God (cf. Job 9:35), he would still find himself silenced. Zophar adds further fuel to the fire by stating, "Know therefore that God exacteth of thee less thine iniquity deserveth" In other words, God had forgotten about a portion of his iniquity. Job on the other hand complained that God searches out and mercilessly marks his every sin (cf. Job 16:14), afflicting him out of proportion of his iniquities. Zophar however, ventures to modify his two other friends' theory of direct ratio-but in the opposite direction from Job. The climax of the first cycle of condemnation ends with the pivotal statement, "Know therefore that God exacteth of thee less than thine iniquity

deserveth." As far as Job's three friends were concerned, he did not even receive full punishment for his
perceived misdeeds.

Throughout his painful ordeal Job continued to long
for a divine advocate and probed much deeper into the
mystery of godliness than his three friends, whose
responses continued to degenerate into irrelevant
harangues of the woes of the wicked and in no way
provided any insight to his situation. He remains
starved for understanding and seeks pity from his
fellow human beings, but finds them incompassionate.
At this juncture Job realized that what his soul really
craved was divine, rather than human vindication. The
hope of a divine vindicator which had been gathering
strength in his spirit impelled him to cry out, "For I
know that my redeemer liveth, and that he shall stand
at the latter day upon the earth" (Job 19:25). Job saw the
office of Redeemer as his next of kin and acknowledged
that it was His responsibility to restore his fortunes,
liberty and name. Deep within his spirit Job somehow
receives the assurance that even though all earthly kin
might have disowned him, his divine Kinsman was
prepared to own him and speak the last word in his
case.

Despite the insensitive rebuffs on the part of his
close friends, Job refused to be driven to reactionary

extremes by the pressure of debate. Instead, he achieved a penetratingly spiritual analysis of the ungodly by realizing that they are without God in the world, which means that not only will they suffer eternal damnation, but that they also have no divine refuge in present trouble (Job 27:9, 10). Job's friends should have realized by his persistent crying to God for respite, their identification of him with the godless was incorrect.

After concluding the verbal engagement with his friends, Job's engagement with God comes to the fore. In a final monologue he summarizes his cause, reflecting on the close covenant relationship with himself and God and the blessedness of those days. Job was actively engaged in civil and judicial affairs and visualized himself as the celebrated champion of the poor and the oppressed. He recognized himself as beloved comforter who was denied a fair hearing by friends and somehow the friendly favor of God had turned into cruelty (Job 30:16-23). Far more distressing to the patriarch than the cruelty of men was that of God (Job 30:21). In Job's own estimation, God persecuted him with physical afflictions continually, humiliatingly, mercilessly, violently and unto the grave. Though at this juncture he fails to pursue the logical implications and to pursue previously expressed thoughts concerning divine wisdom, it brings home the fact about his humanity. He concludes his lament with a melancholy cry and with death fever consuming his frame, he plays beforehand a dirge against the day of his burying.

Protestation of innocence had been Job's main burden from the inception of his afflictions and elaborately formulated it becomes the climax of his peroration and concludes that his Sovereign has visited him with the curses rather than the blessings of the covenant (cf Deuteronomy 28:18,31,35). God seemed to have forsaken the Master's role as protector and strangely turned enemy against an obedient vassal. The picture appears to be that of a covenant vassal protesting his faithfulness to the various stipulations laid on him. He begins by disclaiming private sins of the heart – lust (Job 31:1), vain deceit (Job 31:5) and covetousness (Job 32:7). By so doing, he displays profound spirituality into God's law (cf. Sermon on the Mount Matthew 5; 6; 7). By these references to the penal sanctions of the covenant, Job expertly solemnizes his oaths of innocence. Mingled with his reverential fear of his Judge, is his confident longing to stand before Him. The charge of hypocrisy and secret sin that his friends brought against him, for want of evidence are now contradicted by his protestations and directly repudiated by his denial of concealed sin in his relations with God, his enemies and strangers.

As the drama escalates, a young man named Elihu, apparently a member of the larger audience attending the debate of the masters, suddenly comes forward and presents his theodicy. What provoked Elihu to instruct his elders was the failure to answer satisfactorily Job's defiant protests against God. But yet they condemned Job. He saw the friends' charge of hypocrisy as a shameful cover for their logical theological deficiencies. They failed to prove him wrong in his aspersions against divine justice. In Elihu's estimation the inglorious performance of the counselors demonstrated a lack of wisdom despite their age (Job 32:9,12,15,16), while he on the other hand claims understanding, despite his youth (Job 32:6b, 10). With the compulsion of a spirit bursting with knowledge of the mystery the sages found so perplexing, young Elihu while not condemning Job, hints at the overestimation of his righteousness and provides a strong defense of divine justice.

After Elihu's address, God appeared to Job in a whirlwind and challenged him concerning his sense of estrangement from his Creator. God accused Job of darkening counsel by words without knowledge, that is, instead of explaining the reason for the divine dealings and vindicating God, Job made false accusations against Him and His government. Job was suddenly afforded the opportunity to present his case in the divine court, but after a series of questions from God, he was rendered unable to speak, as he had bragged about in the discourse with his friends. As the questioning intensified, Job finally answered in a manner indicating that his self-righteousness had become a thing to be abhorred. He confessed, "I know that thou canst do everything, and that no thought can be witholden from thee. Who is he that hideth counsel without knowledge? Therefore have I uttered that I understood not; things too wonderful for me, which I knew not" (Job 42:1-2). Job came to the understanding that finite man may not pose as arbiter, for in God and His ways there is mystery beyond human comprehension. But, in all likelihood, one of the most important things Job declared at this juncture were the words, "I have heard of thee by the hearing of the ear: but now mine eyes seeth thee" (Job 42:5). If Job had any misunderstandings about the person of God, he was now enlightened by the fact that he had heard of Him "by the hearing of the ear: but now my eyes seeth thee." The theophany was a transforming experience, illuminating all other divine revelation previously transmitted to Job. By this new revelation, he finds again the way of wisdom and cries out, "Wherefore I abhor myself and repent in dust and ashes" (Job 42:6). Job's confession became the counterbalance of his former complaint and acknowledges the rebelliousness that began with such a complaint. By this unreserved commitment of himself to his Lord, one made while he was still in the throes of his sufferings, not having either received explanation of the mystery of the past or promise of the future, he displayed himself as a true covenant servant, ready to serve God whatever the cost might be. The confession therefore marks his final "bruising" by Satan and the final vindication of God's redemptive power.

Even though God rebuked Job for contending with him, He called Job His servant and acknowledged that in comparison with his three friends he had spoken right things. God knew that the unwise words Job uttered were done under great duress, suffering and satanic pressure – things spoken in heated debate, which he would not have uttered under normal circumstances. With the test now over, God healed Job of his affliction and Satan was defeated. All of his brethren, his sisters and former acquaintances returned to him and partook of Job's hospitality. The final verdict evidenced that "God blessed the latter end of Job more than his beginning, for he had fourteen thousand sheep, and six thousand camels, and a thousand yoke of oxen, and a thousand she asses. He also had seven sons and three daughters" (Job 42:12-13).

History recognizes Job as one of the most patient and God-fearing of all ages. His life stands as an example for all Christians to patiently endure suffering while being tried under the attack of Satan. But one important thing that we might glean from Job's suffering was his capacity to wait for a change in his situation. In addition to seeking God and committing his cause to Him (Job 5:8), he declared, *"All the days of my appointed time will I wait till my change comes"* (Job 14:14b). Victory over adversity was in large part due to Job's capacity to wait until his change came. In other words he did not throw in the towel and give up when the going got rough. But instead, he looked for meaning in his suffering.

In his best-selling book, *Man's Search For Meaning*, Victor Frankl, the world famous Viennese author and psychiatrist, provides concrete evidence from his three year incarceration in Nazi concentration camps during World war II, that even when everything is taken from an individual, they are still left with the last of the human freedoms — to choose one's attitude in any set of circumstances, to choose one's own way.

During his imprisonment in bestial concentration camps at Auswich, Poland, and a camp associated with Dachau, in Germany, Frankl found himself stripped to naked existence. His father, mother, brother and his wife died in camps or were sent to gas ovens by Hitler's murderous henchmen, so that except for his sister, his entire family perished in these camps. During his baptism by fire, he learned that every circumstance conspires to make a prisoner lose their hold when all the familiar goals in life were snatched away and the only thing remaining is "the last of the human freedoms"— the ability to choose one's attitude in any given set of circumstances. He discovered, therefore, that the key to survival depended on a prisoner's ability to make sense out of his or her apparently senseless suffering.

Frankl reminds us of something that we know all too well, but choose to ignore, that being, that suffering is a permanent fixture of the human landscape. He believes that human life under any circumstances, never ceases to have meaning and this infinite meaning of life includes suffering, dying, privation and death. Frankl advocates that *to live is to suffer and to survive is to find meaning in one's suffering.* If there is a purpose in life after all, there must be purpose in suffering and dying. The fact that we frequently refuse to embrace suffering as a part of life, makes it much more difficult to cultivate a positive orientation towards the future. However, in order to discover meaning for our lives, even when we find ourselves confronted by the worst kind of adversity, we must subscribe to the exhortation of our Lord to take up our cross — to practice endurance until change comes. Each of us under the most horrific circumstances must decide what will ultimately become of us — mentally and spiritually. And it is *only* through the activation of our inner resources that we are raised above any outer situation that might threaten our existence.

Frankl's outlook on life resonates with a most profound truth found in the Bible, that being, that one's inner worth is anchored in higher, more spiritual things and cannot be shaken by external situations. He contends that deposited within each human being is an inner liberty — a spiritual greatness, which has the potential to penetrate the enveloping gloom and transcend our hopeless, meaningless world, whereby we develop the capacity to hear a victorious "Yes" in answer to questions of our existence and ultimate purpose in life. The very same "Yes" that Job heard because he was determined to wait until his change came. This is the very same "Yes" that echoes within our spirit when we invoke the words of the apostle John, "Greater is he that is in you, than he that is in the world" (1 John 4:4).

The Bible is fraught with examples of instances where individuals developed the capacity to deepen their spiritual lives, even though they were subjected to the most horrific circumstances. By engaging in spiritual defiance they developed the capacity to retreat from the chaos of the human experience to a life of inner riches and spiritual freedom — a freedom that is always discovered when we entrust our circumstances to the capable shoulders of Almighty God and *wait* until our change comes.

Chapter Five

Unshackled
(Luke 5:1-20)

๕๛

Jesus had a knack for making unexpected incursions into strange and unusual places. His foray into Gadara, a city located twenty miles southeast of the Sea of Galilee was one such undertaking. None of his disciples could quite comprehend at the time why for no apparent reason their Master chose to embark on a journey off the beaten path into hostile territory. It was not until later that they gained a full understanding that our Lord was always intent on seeking out oppressed members of the human family wherever they might be found.

Luke reports that when Jesus and his disciples had crossed over the Sea of Galilee to the other side, they arrived in the country of the Gadarenes. After they got out of the ship, a man who had his dwelling place in or among the tombs met them. He had reached a point so extreme that he was forced out of society and necessitated that he be bound with chains. But even the chains, which were used to restrain him, were of no use, because he possessed superhuman power and broke them in pieces. No one had strength enough to tame this wild beast of a man.

Throughout the night and day the high decibel shrieks of the madman pierced the atmosphere and all the while he relentlessly slashed himself with stones. Blood oozed from every imaginable part of his body, rendering him a pitiful sight. As he convulsed wildly among the tombstones, he was stopped in his tracks by a familiar figure. To his utter amazement, the Majesty of heaven enfleshed in the garb of humanity was unexpectedly on his territory. Recognizing Jesus from afar off, he ran towards him, fell down and worshipped him and cried out with a loud voice, "Jesus, thou son of the most high God? I adjure thee by God that thou torment me not." Jesus responded, "Come out of the man, thou unclean spirit." He then questioned him asking, "What is thy name." The man responded saying, "My name is legion: for we are many." The name legion is indicative of the number six thousand, which represents the compliment of soldiers in a Roman legion. In this instance, it indicated that the man was possessed by six thousand demons. "We are many." From all indications, one demon appeared to be the spokesperson for the six thousand that had taken possession of the man.

The response of the madman to Jesus' appearance is a remarkable indication of supernatural knowledge. The afflicted man was well aware of the name of Jesus and his Deity, although this, as it appears, was his first encounter with Christ. Such knowledge is proof that the man was not merely insane; but that he was indwelt by satanic powers that were intimately familiar with the true identity of Christ.

After hearing Jesus' command, the demons implored him that he would not send them out of the country, but rather permit them to enter a herd of about two thousand swine that was feeding on the hillside. The significance of the phrase "Out of the country," is to be seen in Luke's reference to the abyss (Luke 8:31). The demons feared being returned to the place of detention to remain in a disembodied state until the judgment.

After the demons entered the swine the herd ran violently down the steep hillside into the sea and drowned. The question persistently provoked by this passage concerns the ethical propriety of Jesus' actions resulting as it did in the destruction of the property of others. A common answer has always been that Jews had no right to own pigs and Christ thus rebuked their breaking of the Mosaic Law. But since the region of Decapolis contained a mixed population of both Jews and Gentiles, there is no absolute assurance that the owners were Jews or that this was the purpose of Christ's action. The passage is quite clear that he did not command the demons to enter the swine; he permitted them. In all reality, it was the demons, not the Lord, who caused the destruction.

When the people who cared for the swine saw what had taken place, they ran into the city and reported what Jesus had done. The curious townspeople came out to see Jesus and also the man who was at one time possessed by demons. When they observed the man sitting in his right mind, they were afraid. They were not actually afraid of the cured man, but of the remarkable power that was able to cure him. As the keepers of the swineherd continued to proclaim what had transpired, the townspeople begged Jesus to depart from among them. They were aware of the supernatural power in the person of Christ, but totally unaware of his infinite love and mercy.

Not being one to force himself into a community that refused to extend the welcome carpet to him, Jesus retraced his steps back to the seashore and got back into the boat. At this juncture the man that he had cured implored the Master that he be allowed to go along with him and his disciples. However, Jesus responded telling him, "Go home to thy friends, and tell them how great things the Lord hath done for thee and had compassion on thee." It might appear at first glance that Jesus was being insensitive by not permitting the man to become part of his roving band of disciples. But while the townspeople treated Jesus as persona non grata, the cured man was the perfect evangelist to remain in the community to bear witness of God's love to the unlovely population. A basic principle underlies Christ's command — man is not delivered from bondage for his own enjoyment of God-given freedom. But rather that he may give testimony concerning the power of the divine Deliverer.

Jesus arrived in Gadara uninvited and despite the supernatural feat he demonstrated in the midst of the people; he was unceremoniously ushered out of town like someone afflicted with a incurable plague. He certainly had to have had some inkling concerning the way things would eventually turn out. So why was he so determined to venture into unfriendly territory anyway?

After reading Luke's narrative of the poor man's plight, we are able glean one perspective of the sufferer's dilemma. But it is a well-known fact that when a member of the human family is burdened by oppression, suffering is usually pervasive throughout the entire family unit. In this vein, when we put the man's situation in its human context, we might be able to gain further insight as to why Jesus journeyed to Gadara.

There is no indication in Luke's report that the man had a wife or children. But it is quite possible that he had parents that were still alive. Like normal run-of-the-mill parents they undoubtedly loved their son dearly. He could very well have been the eldest sibling who was destined to someday take over the reigns of the family when the patriarch passed away. Both parents did their dead-level best to raise him in the best possible way that they could. His development appeared quite normal, but unexpectedly things went awry and the boy morphed into a raving lunatic. His behavior became so violent that they were compelled to have him consigned to the local graveyard on the outskirts of town. Living out his remaining days among the tombstones, he became for all practical purposes the living dead.

Again, it is pure conjecture, but the boy's parents might have on numerous occasions ventured out to the local graveyard under the cover of darkness and watched their son from the distance as he uncontrollably inflicted painful wounds to his body. The questions swirling around inside their heads were many and caused their hearts to splinter as they became engulfed by the kind of pain that frequently pushed them to the point of becoming themselves deranged.

As Jesus utilized his spiritual radar to probe the length and breadth of the universe to discern where human suffering was taking place, his spirit rested on the pain emanating from Gadara — the pain of the young man and his traumatized family members. This was undoubtedly the main reason that he felt compelled to inject himself into hostile territory. Throughout the brief three or so years of his earthly ministry he always demonstrated that he was primarily concerned about the worth and dignity of human beings and was bent on reconciling back into the mainstream of society those individuals who found themselves marginalized and ostracized in any way.

Jesus' foray into Gadara to unshackle a demon-possessed child of God from chains and sickness mirrors his foray from his heavenly throne, in order that he might unshackle humanity from the burden of sin. His subsequent march to Calvary where he was put to death on a crude Roman cross as the atoning sacrifice for the sin of the entire world, demonstrated that he was willing to descend to the lowest depths to meet human-kind in whatever condition and situation they found themselves, in order that he might reconcile them with the Love of their lives. And because Jesus gave his all for us in order that we might experience unshackling from sin, we are compelled to spread the message of how good God has been to us. This is the motivation that prompted John to declare, "In this is love, not that we love God but that he loved us and sent his Son to be the expiation for our sin" (1 John 4:10).

God continues to seek out men and women in the most unusual conditions and circumstances, thereby giving testimony to the fact that He is not only a God for us, but a God with us. It matters not what the magnitude of our oppression might be or to whatever far-flung corner of existence sin might have estranged us, God's love could reach and unshackle us from any predicament that might consign us to hell on earth. He only demands that we recognize our need for liberation and surrender our lives to the Lordship of His only begotten Son, Jesus.

Chapter Six

Is Anything Too Hard For God?
(Genesis 18:9-15; 21:1-3)

ह‍ॐ✦

I f a ninety-year-old woman announced that she would give birth to a baby boy in the near future, the average individual would humor her to her face and buckle over with laughter the instant that she was out of sight. This was exactly the response of Abram's wife Sarai, when she overheard a divine messenger informing her husband that she was destined to give birth to a son within the upcoming year.

Jehovah called Abram to a new station in life by telling him, "Get thee out of thy country and from thy kindred and from thy father's house, unto a land that I will shew thee" (Genesis 12:1). The biblical report indicates that before migrating to Palestine, Abram had two homes. He spent his early years in Ur, in addition to a subsequent long season in Haran (Genesis 11:31). On account of the divine mandate, he was compelled to sever ties with friends, neighbors and kindred that were left behind when he departed Ur and yet again others when he departed Haran. In each case, the threefold tie of land, people and kindred were ruptured to face the uncertainties of the future, in order that he might submit himself completely to Jehovah's will. While Jehovah did not name the land at the time of the call, nor did He describe it to Abram, He knew that in Abram He had found the man for His purpose, one who could be subjected to heavy strains and one who would regard doing His will at the most important thing in life.

After receiving his call, God fortified Abram with covenant promises of prosperity by telling him, "I will make of thee a great nation, and I will bless thee and make thy name great; and thou shalt be a blessing: And I will bless them that bless thee, and curse him that curseth thee: and in thee shall all families of the earth be blessed" (Genesis 12:2-3). The promise of divine blessing guaranteed Abram everything he could desire. He felt assured that his every need would be supplied and even hostile neighbors eventually came to regard him as the leader of God's people. Through him would come blessings to all peoples and his name would be honored and revered throughout the earth. Today, he is recognized and honored as a pillar of the Christian, Jewish and Moslem religions.

Abram was seventy-five years old when he departed Haran with his wife Sarai and Lot his brother's son and all their earthly possessions and they journeyed to the land of Canaan. As he passed through the land and came to Sechem, the Lord appeared unto him and said, "Unto thy seed will I give this land" It was at this location Abram built an altar to God (Genesis 12:7).

Throughout his life Abram manifested a strong faith in God. During the early years it was easy to let this trust shine forth in hours of triumph. When he called to memory God's wondrous promise to him, he took comfort from this declaration that their fulfillment was destined to be through his own seed (Genesis 15:1-21). But as the years slipped on by and he became an old man and realized that he was nearing the end of his life, he was tempted to become discouraged. His faith in the promise wavered and he questioned as to how God would fulfill His promise when all the evidence of human physiology indicated that time was against him.

In deep throes of doubt God exhorted Abram to put away fear by trusting fully in His promises. He exhorted the old man, "Fear not ......I am thy shield and thy exceeding great reward" (Genesis 15:1). The figure of God as a shield was calculated to provide hope, courage and faith to a wavering soul. But despite the divine exhortation, Abram felt the need to have before his eyes the certainty of a tangible reward that would bring to him the fullest of joys.

As time passed Abram continued to waver in his faith and voiced the opinion wishing that his servant Eliezer of Damascus would become his heir. But God assured him that Eliezer would not be his heir and that a son of his own begetting would be born to bring a rich fulfillment of every prediction (Genesis 15:2-4). In moments of peril and despair he was instructed to anchor his very existence in God's protection, God's fulfillment of His promises and the unlimited number of his descendants. He was called to a challenge of sublime trust. But, despite his intermittent doubts he knew that God could be trusted. Even though no child had materialized in his home, he knew that God could fill the earth with those who would someday look back to him as father. Because of the exercise of his faith, God counted it to him as righteousness.

Inasmuch as Abram displayed enormous faith in the promises of Jehovah, he soon fell into slippery places as the years rolled on and no child materialized to brighten the family home. Jehovah had been specific in His promise of an heir (cf. Genesis 15:4), but with the passing years the discrepancy between the promise and the existing circumstances became more and more baffling. Sarai was barren and to be childless was a calamity and a disgrace for a Hebrew wife, who was regarded as a social nonentity because she had no child and therefore no status. The burden of the stigma eventually became so overbearing for her that she began complaining to Abram for not having given birth to any offspring of her own and implored him that she be allowed to produce children through her maid Hagar.

In their own minds, Abram and Sarai believed that they were helping God to fulfill His promise. Both knew the teachings of Genesis 2:24 and realized that husbands and wives were required to conform to that high standard. For a man to take a secondary wife or concubine was sinful. Yet, in an attempt to provide a way for God to carry out His prediction, Sarai was willing to disregard the divine edict and give her female slave, Hagar, to Abram, in the hope that she might bear a son for the family. This is proof positive that when men and women allow their faith in God's promises to break down, they inevitably resort to human contrivance. The Egyptian slave was brought into Abraham's tent that the family night be **built**. But discord and heartache were the ensuing tragic consequences.

Despite the fact that Abram and Sarai were expected to hold themselves to a higher standard by not acting in accordance with the customs of other nations of their day, Abram succumbed to his wife's suggestion. Abram the friend of God exercised a richer faith and was bound by a purer code. Nevertheless, he acquiesced to his wife's dictates and invited Hagar into his tent.

From the very moment Hagar discovered that she was pregnant she began to despise her mistress. Additionally, Sarai became embittered against her maid. All three persons in the triangle suffered on account of the unsound decision to birth a heir through Hagar. Sarai blamed Abram for the whole mess. But the old boy had merely carried out his wife's suggestion. Jealousy completely changed the atmosphere of the home environment, causing it to verge on the point of breakup.

Refusing to put up with Hagar's insolence any longer, Sarai began to ill treat her slave. The persecution meted out to Hagar became so intolerable that it drove her away from her mistress. Passionate jealousy set the two women against each other and Abram was not much help to either of them as conditions grew worse with each passing moment. In desperation, Hagar fled Abram's household in the direction of her homeland, Egypt. She was legally a slave and had no right to run away. But since flight seemed to be the only source of relief, she acted on that option with the hope of finding respite in her old country. When she reached Shur (*the wall*), she paused for a while before crossing the border. This demarcation line is aptly named because the Egyptians maintained a wall or strong line of forts to protect Egypt from invaders from the east.

In the tranquility of the cool wilderness Hagar found herself confronted by the angel of Jehovah to the earth (Genesis 16:7-14). It was a moment of unusual significance in her life, because the angel was not a created being, but none other than Jehovah manifesting Himself to Hagar. He identified Himself with Jehovah; spoke and acted with God's authority and is spoken of as God, or Jehovah.

The angel's heartening words to Hagar instructed her to return to the hard situation she left behind and take up her burden once more. She was exhorted to wait for the fulfillment of the divine plan and look for the day when her son Ismael, would become the head of an important tribe. The name Ishmael means *God heareth* and he was to be a "wild ass of a man," with strength and daring and a ferocious disposition. He would live wild and unshackled out in the wilderness, without friends or loyalties. And his descendants were destined to grow into a mighty horde of Bedouins, wild free, treacherous, reckless men, roaming the open spaces of the desert.

Hagar was overjoyed to recognize God in her experience and to see Him as a gracious, kindly and thoughtful observer of a poor slave in dire need. As such, she responded to the divine directive with reverent faith. The well where she had her encounter with Jehovah was renamed *Beer-lahai-roi,* an indication of the fact that she was moved mightily by the realization that she had been in the very presence of Almighty God and was able to survive. It is believed that the well was in the vicinity of Kadesh (cf. Genesis 16:14), about fifty miles south of Beersheba. Hagar's son was born and the name Ishmael was given to him by Abram, then eighty-six years old.

Thirteen years later at the ripe old age of ninety-nine, Almighty God (*'El Shadai*) appeared to Abram with a reassurance, a challenge and a richer promise. God reminded him that His covenant was with him and that He would make him a father of many nations. He was also informed that his name was now being changed from Abram to Abraham. The name Abram means *exalted father,* whereas Abraham means *father of a multitude.* He was additionally informed that the name of his wife Sarai was being changed to Sarah and that she would be blessed to have a son and that she would become a mother of nations and kings would ensue from her. The name Sarai means *princely*. Sarah means *mother of princes*, which was indicative of her future status. Abraham fell on his face and laughed at the report, questioning whether a child was to be born to him and his wife when they were one hundred years old and ninety years old respectively. Believing that it was physiologically impossible for him and Sarah to produce a son of their own at such an advanced stage in life, Abraham continued to voice the desire of Ishmael becoming his heir. God again reassured Abraham that his wife Sarah would give birth to a son and the child's name would be called Isaac. God indicated that He would establish an everlasting covenant with the patriarch and with his seed after him.

Unexpectedly one day, three divine messengers showed up at Abraham's home in the plains of Mamre as he sat in his tent door in the heat of the day. It was customary for desert dwellers to sit under the door flap of tents for shade and to eat the noon meal when the sun was hottest and the heat oppressive. When he saw the three messengers, he ran from his tent to meet them and bowed himself toward the ground. He then requested that they allow him to provide them with water to wash the desert sand off their feet and prepare a meal for them. After they consented to partake of Abraham's hospitality, he instructed Sarah to prepare bread for them while he went to the herd and selected a calf, which he gave to one of his servants to slaughter and prepare for the visitors. The servant complied with Abraham's request and prepared a sumptuous meal for the three mysterious visitors to his compound.

After partaking of the meal that was set before them, the visitors questioned Abraham concerning the whereabouts of Sarah and he informed them that she was in her tent. One of them informed the old patriarch that in the upcoming year Sarah would give birth to the long-awaited son that was promised them. Sarah overheard the announcement and knowing that she was beyond the age of conception, laughed within herself, saying, "After I am waxed old shall I have pleasure, my lord being old also" (Genesis 18:12). One of the messengers ascribed to as "The Lord," questioned Abraham as to why Sarah laughed at the announcement that she would bear a child in her old age. He went further to question Abraham, **"Is anything too hard for the Lord?"** (Genesis 18:14). The Lord again restated the oft-repeated promise of a son to Abraham, telling him that at the appointed time He would return and Sarah would give birth to a son. Fearing divine retribution on account of her disbelief, Sarah denied laughing. However, remaining true to His promise, the Lord visited

Sarah as promised and she conceived and bore Abraham a son whom he named Isaac (Genesis 21:1-2). Every covenant prediction was to have divine fulfillment through this son of Abraham. When Sarah held the babe in her arms, her joy knew no bounds. For many months she lived for that sacred moment. She exclaimed: **"God had made me to laugh; everyone that heareth will laugh with me"** (Genesis 21:6). For the neighbors it would be the laughter of good-natured surprise coupled with genuine delight and hearty felicitation. For Sarah it was the joyous laughter of wondrous realization, because she knew full well that she held in her arms God's gift to the world.

Abraham was compelled to wait for almost a quarter of a century before he finally realized the promise of God. On several occasions he became spiritually and emotionally deflated by the long wait, causing God's word to lose its resonance and relevance. However, Abraham's travails reveal several insights that might help us in our own spiritual development as we continue our journey up life's road. The important thing we need to realize is, *God's delays are not God's denial.* Despite the fact that there might be a long interval subsequent to the time He makes a promise to us and the time when the promise is actually fulfilled, He will *always* honor His word. The Bible tells us that God honors His word above His name. Therefore, we must always trust His word, despite any delays that we might be compelled to endure before experiencing His promise.

The second insight we notice from Abraham's situation is the fact that being compelled to wait for long periods before receiving God's promises oftentimes tend to breed a sense of despair. On several occasions Abraham complained to God about not receiving the promise that was made to him. By subjecting him to a long period of waiting God was teaching Abraham patience.

Patience comes from the ancient root word *patior*, which means to suffer. In order to learn patience, we are taught the important lesson of not rebelling against every hardship that we are subjected to in life. Jesus reminds us in the Bible: "In this life you will *suffer* tribulation, but be of good cheer for I have overcome the world" (John 16:33). Jesus never told us that we would avoid tribulation. He told us that we would suffer tribulation. He also reminds us that tribulation need not have the last word, because on account of his status as Savior, he *overcame* the world. He stated at another time, "All power is given unto me in heaven and earth (Matthew 28:18). God does not save us *from* tribulation, He saves us *in* tribulation. So, when we develop the capacity to discover God's Spirit at work in our lives, even in those instances when our world is in flux and our future in great doubt, this is a unique opportunity to learn the important lesson that absolutely nothing lies outside the realm of God's mercy. As such, we do not have to remain immobilized at the station of adversity, because God avails us power through Christ to move beyond any form of adversity. Acknowledging this important reality inoculates us against becoming cynical and aggressive when the shallowness of taking the easy path wears through.

A third insight that we learn from Abraham's situation is the fact that we must refrain from looking at external or environmental factors as the barometer of God's promises. Both Abraham and Sarah were close to one hundred years old before God made the birth of Isaac a reality in their lives. Both individuals realized that the laws of human physiology were working against them. As such, they believed that it was humanly impossible for a ninety-year plus old woman to give birth to a baby. While this phenomenon might not be an everyday occurrence, God promised Abraham that Sarah would give birth to a child of her own and because God gave His word He had to deliver on His promise. God had to prove to both individuals that He is the Supreme Ruler over all creation and creation is under His subjection and not the other way round. Therefore, despite the fact that Sarah was approaching the hundred-year mark, He was still the Creator of all life and His creative activity is in no way limited by environmental factors.

Abraham is recognized as a pillar of the Christian religion for his enormous reservoir of faith. But his enormous capital of faith did not come easy. His ascendancy to the status of one who personifies faith came through an enormous amount of *spiritual pruning*. And this is the fourth insight.

Jesus informed his disciples that while they might have been intimately related to him as branches were to a vine, they occasionally needed to be pruned, in order to bear more fruit (see John 15:1-5). In the act of pruning, a vinedresser cuts away all of the dead and non-functional branches from a vine. He clips or removes all of the unproductive parts of the plant that diminishes vitality, in order that the productive capacity of the vine might be concentrated in those areas that would produce the greatest abundance of grapes.

Pruning is painful and we do not readily welcome this activity of God in our lives. But, God knows that it is essential that He strip away unproductive pursuits and habits to which we are attached and which squander vital resources that not only weakens us spiritually, but ultimately diminishes our productive or fruit-bearing capacity. Abraham and Sarah became engaged in the futile exercise of producing a son through Hagar, believing that they were *helping* God make His promise become a reality. In so doing, they squandered much productive energy and brought enormous pain on themselves, because this was not God's design in fulfilling His promise in their lives. God had to put Abraham and Sarah through His finishing school and prune them until they learned the painful lesson that as the heavens are higher than the earth, so are His ways higher that our ways and His thoughts higher than our thoughts. Abraham and Sarah learned the important lesson that God is no killjoy who subjects His children to discomfort for the mere pleasure of it. But more importantly, they learned that pruning is the art of preparation, whereby God refashions His beloved children to operate at higher levels of faithfulness and productivity.

The last, but certainly not the least insight we might glean from Abraham's travail, is the fact that pruning is essential for perfection. God needed to perfect Abraham in order that he might stand out as a stellar example for all humanity. But before becoming God's poster boy of faith, he first had to be perfected.

In addition to being beautiful and expensive, diamonds are the hardest substances on earth. Geologist and gemologists report that even the smallest diamond takes at least a million years to be perfected. Diamonds are formed from coal or graphite. Before becoming the much sought after gems, coal is first subjected to enormous amounts of heat and pressure while lying within the bowels of the earth. The synergy of heat and pressure to which coal is subjected eventually produce beautiful and expensive diamonds. The very same holds true for us as human beings. Before God could utilize us for Kingdom business, He must first perfect us by subjecting us to enormous amounts of pressure.

God made Abraham aware of the fact that he would have a son that would ensue from his loins. But when the promise took a long time coming, he wavered and wished that Ishmael would be his heir. We oftentimes behave the very same way when we do not receive God's promises according to our perceived time schedule. Like Abraham, He must first teach us the important lesson of synchronizing our lives with His time schedule.

While waiting on God, we need to realize that we are compelled to deal with two kinds of time. The first is *chronological* or clock time, which comes from the Greek word *chronos*. The second kind of time is *kairos*.

This is a New Testament Greek word that has to do with opportune moments that are ripe for their intended purpose. In this vein, even when we are subjected to long stretches of adversity along life's road, God desires that we develop the capacity to discern that something good is happening amidst all the disruptions. We might learn in hindsight from Abraham that God could very well be working out His purpose in our days. Even though our days might be painful, there is a greater purpose in the pain. By understanding this important fact, we might come to the full understanding that our painful experience is not something to manipulate or get through as quickly as possible. But instead, we might come to understand that our pain-drenched days is nothing more than God's arena where like a beautiful and expensive diamond in the rough, He is subjecting us to pressure, in order that He might perfect us. The real truth of the matter is that God calls us to trust Him in all circumstances, because He is always making something good out of our hardships in ways that we might not yet fully comprehend. It is by trusting His guiding hand not only in blissful moments, but also when we are subjected to shadows of disappointment and darkness. Because God has our best interest at heart, we must always hold our heads high into the future and straighten our drooping shoulders and proclaim within our spirit **that nothing is too hard for God.**

Chapter Seven

Morning Joy
(Psalm 30:5)

ॐ

The dawning of morning has a mesmerizing effect on nature. If anyone had the blessed opportunity to be present in a wild life nature preserve as the rising sun crept slowly over the horizon to illuminate the eastern sky, they would witness a sacred benediction as thousands of birds simultaneously took flight into the sky in a glorious salute to the birthing of another day, while raising their voice in song. They would also notice beautiful flowers effortlessly swing wide their colorful petals to embrace the energizing force of golden rays of sunlight that were being splashed across their surfaces.

The response of the human spirit to the charismatic rush of God's Holy Spirit in many ways mirror the response of nature's fauna and flora to the arrival of morning. The advent of the Spirit gives birth to a new vitality that pulses through everything, rekindling hope that had long since grown cold from suffering and despair. It also marks that moment when new meaning is given the ancient words: "The eyes of the blind are opened, the captives are set free and the acceptable year of the Lord become literal truth!" This reality impels the human spirit to respond with joy over the fact that no matter how dark days might appear, the redemptive impulse of God remains present and operative in human life.

The preceding chapters remind us in stark terms that suffering is a variable of human life. One writer described suffering as *"The dark night of the soul."* The Bible is fraught with metaphorical language and there is a high probability that the writer's description of suffering was influenced by Psalm 30, which suggests that difficulties occurring in one's life are in many ways a nighttime experience that darkens the climate of the human spirit and produces weeping which ceases at the dawning of morning, or the time when liberation comes.

Psalm 30 indicates that suffering is a death-producing power that malevolently injects its jangled discords into the harmonious symphony of life. A person can, despite the fact that he or she is actively living and breathing, nevertheless be subjected to enormous pain, anxiety, despair, or lethargy that escalates to the point where the individual's existence can no longer be truly called life. This is so, because when a person becomes the recipient of enormous suffering, death is at work in their lives. As is the case of the personalities discussed in the previous six chapters, anyone who is subjected to suffering is said to be in the clutches of death. Therefore, anyone who is liberated by the power of God is rescued from the power of death and this experience gives birth to a joyous response. Joy is the immediate echo of the human soul to an act of God, or the validating response of the soul to God's omnipotence. But more importantly, while joy is a response or echo of the soul to God's omnipotence over tribulation, it is also the reigning assumption that in God's economy suffering does not have the last word.

There are important reasons for the eruption of joy when God's Holy Spirit makes contact with the human spirit. The first reason is the fact that we become intimately aware of our belovedness.

On the occasion of our Lord's baptism in the Jordan River and yet again at his transfiguration on Mount Tabor, God spoke directly to the assembled crowd (at Jordan) and to Peter, James and John (at the mountain),

115

informing them of the belovedness of His son. God repeatedly reminds us of our own belovedness through-out the Bible. In the writings of the apostle John, the author declares, "Behold what manner of love the Father has bestowed upon us that we should be called the children of God..." The apostle goes further to state: "*Beloved,* now we are the children of God; and it has not yet been revealed what we shall be, but we know that when He is revealed, we shall be like Him, for we shall see Him as He is (1 John 3:1-2). The arresting language employed by John indicates with all unmistakable clarity that our heavenly Father recognizes *all* of His children as beloved creatures.

The number one problem plaguing humanity and producing a deficit of joy on planet earth is the inability of individuals to recognize their inherent belovedness on the part of God. This is evidenced by the prevalence of celebrity worship where untold millions are unhappy with their own creation and attempt to live their lives vicariously through some famous personality. Many are so dissatisfied with their physical appearance that they subject themselves to cosmetic surgery, in an attempt to alter their appearance and achieve a different look. Some even venture so far as attempting to reconstruct their appearance to replicate the features of the celebrity they have grown to idolize. The inability of individuals to recognize their inherent belovedness by God causes them to feel alienated from the Love of their lives. As such, they go through life with a gnawing sense of emptiness on the inside that causes them to grasp at every passing fad they believe would somehow endow them with a permanent sense of identity. The corrective for this dilemma is the need for each of us to embrace the truth that God loves each individual human life with an undying love. In his writings, Augustine, the great Bishop of Hippo fingered it, "Thou hast made us for thyself, O God and our hearts are restless until they come to rest in thee."

The truth that we are afforded the opportunity to recapture a sense of our belovedness on the part of God is evidenced by several passages throughout the Bible. One such example is outlined in John 4, where a Samaritan woman learns the astounding truth about her created identity — the reality of her belovedness.

The spellbinding narrative reports that Jesus was resting at Jacob's well when a woman approached the watering hole with her water jar in the stifling noonday heat. It was the local custom for women to gather at the well to draw water in the cool of the early morning or at dusk when the sun was going down. But to do so at midday when the sun was at the highest point in the sky was highly unusual. He discerned in his spirit that the approaching stranger did not feel quite comfortable among her peers and made the unexpected gesture of asking the woman to give him water to drink. Immediately her curiosity was piqued. She questioned Jesus, "How is it that You, being a Jew, ask a drink from me, a Samaritan woman?" (John 4:9). She was well aware of the existing tribal fault lines between Jews and Samaritans and knew that Jews looked down their noses at Samaritans, because they were relegated to the status of half-breeds who did not subscribe to the Jewish religious faith. As such, she was curious as to why Jesus would even bother to take notice of her. She knew full well that the stranger addressing her had broken through the established barriers of religious tradition; social expectations and gender rules and she probably wondered what trick he had up his sleeve. Maybe he was on the hunt for sexual favors? After all, she knew that in the vast majority of cases the men who addressed her only did so because she was an easy target for their lust.

Jesus could see the wheels turning in the woman's head and knew the thoughts that were going through her curious mind. He responded to her, "If you knew the gift of God, and *who* it is that says to you, 'Give me a drink,' you would have asked Him, and He would have given you living water" (John 4:10).

Playing along with what she thought was an amusing charade by not disclosing her true feeling, the woman responded to Jesus, "Sir, you have nothing to draw with, and the well is deep where then do you get that living water? Are you greater than our father Jacob, who gave us the well, and drank from it himself, as well as his sons and his livestock" (John 4:12). Jesus answered her, "Whoever drinks of this water will thirst again, but whoever drinks of the water that I shall give him will never thirst. But the water that I shall give him will become in him a fountain of living water springing up into everlasting life (John 4:13-14).

After hearing the amazing declaration, the woman requested that Jesus provide her with water, in order that she would not have to return to the well on subsequent occasions. Jesus instructed the woman go and fetch her husband. She responded saying, "I have no husband" Jesus said to her, "You have said well, 'I have no husband,' "for you have had five husbands, and the one whom you now have is not your husband; in that you spoke truly" (John 4:17-18). The woman responded to Jesus' comment informing him that she surmised that he was a prophet and stated that her ancestors signified that they should worship on that very mountain. But yet the Jews indicate that Jerusalem was the place to worship. Jesus responded saying, "Woman, believe Me, the hour is coming when you will neither on this mountain, nor in Jerusalem, worship the Father. You worship what you do not know; we know what we worship, for salvation is of the Jews. But the hour is coming, and now is, when the true worshippers will worship the Father in spirit and in truth; for the Father is seeking such to worship Him. God is Spirit, and those who worship Him must worship Him in spirit and truth (John 4:21-24). The woman responded saying, "I know that the Messiah is coming (who is called Christ) when he comes, He will tell us all things." Jesus declared to the woman saying, "I who speak to you am he" John 4:25-26).

Shortly after making his pronouncement, the disciples of Jesus arrived on the scene and observing the dialogue between Jesus and the woman, enquired as to why he was talking with her. They were aware that such social intercourse went against the grain of society and were obviously curious as to why he would breach historical protocol. At this juncture the woman abandoned her water pot and raced back into the city and announced to the people, "Come see a man who told me all things that I ever did. Could this be the Christ?" After hearing the amazing report, the people went out of the city to see Jesus (John 4:27-30).

Because of his divine personality, Jesus was intimately acquainted with the minutest detail of the woman's life. But his deep compassion for the plight of humanity prevented him from allowing her to continue avoiding the truth, not because he had a penchant for scolding or condemning, but because he was aware of the fact that her promiscuous lifestyle masked the emptiness of her heart. With deep respect and dignity, the Messiah led her to an awakened realization about her true worth and to the presence of God within her. As a result of the experience, she became the object of transformation. Her shame gave birth to jubilant hope when Jesus revealed to her that she was loved and valued by her Creator and her spirit was suddenly illuminated with the shaft of light that was thrown across her path. Recognizing that she was beloved by God, she experienced a sense of wholesomeness that compelled her to rejoin the community from which she was once ostracized.

The interaction of Jesus with the Samaritan woman represented on the individual level a microcosm of his global mission to the entire human family, whereby he might reunite us with the Love of our lives and bring us back into community with the Source of all life.

The Bible indicates that Jesus was motivated by a deep joy that propelled him towards Calvary, whereby he could make atonement for the sins of the entire word. This reality is illuminated by the writer of Hebrew who states: "Wherefore seeing that we are compassed about with so great a cloud of witnesses, let us lay aside every weight, and the sin which doth so easily beset us and let us run with patience the race that is set before us, Looking unto Jesus the author and finisher of our faith; who for the *joy* that was set before him endured the cross, despising the shame, and is set down at the right hand of the throne of God" (Hebrews 12:1-2).

We are intimately familiar with the life of Jesus and how it ended on a hill called Calvary, located outside the massive stone walls of Jerusalem. But despite the biting ridicule and rejection he experienced from malicious religious leaders of his day and the ignominious death he eventually suffered, in order to make atonement for the sins of the world, he still experienced a percolating joy at the core of his personality. This is so because the reigning assumption in his spirit resonated with the truth that his heavenly Father had power over death and the grave. As such, Jesus developed the capacity not only to endure, but also to triumph over the challenges that confronted him in life. By the same token, in order for us to experience joy at the core of our being, the reigning assumption in our spirit must be the recognition that God affords us power to triumph over any situation that might confront us on this side of eternity.

The writer of Hebrews likens life to a race. There are different kinds of races, foot races, horse races, car races, etc. And while each race has its unique characteristics, each has a beginning and an end.

Car racing is quite a popular sport throughout the world that ends with the winner crossing the finishing line greeted by a checkered flag. If we employ car racing as a metaphor for our Lord's journey through life and his capacity to remain joyful, we might say that the most important thing he did was that of keeping his eye on the checkered flag. He kept his eye on the end. He kept his eye on the fact that his heavenly Father had the last word as to how his life would ultimately turn out.

In order for us to remain joyful amidst the trials and tribulations of life, it is essential that we emulate our Lord and keep our eyes on the checkered flag. Jesus told his disciples. "In this life you will suffer tribulation, but be of good *cheer* for I have overcome the world" (John 16:33). Jesus knew that humans oftentimes become disillusioned when despair establishes camp within and alters the geography of our spirit. However, he knew that the antidote to despair is to acknowledge that through his empowerment we are afforded victory over despair. He reminds us that it is resurrection power and not despair that ultimately has the last word. Therefore, by focusing on the end result we too can develop the capacity to endure the hardships of life and visualize ourselves in the winners' circle, because we know what the end result will be when we open ourselves up to the transforming power of God.

Continuing to employ car racing as a metaphor for life, we recognize that most automobile races are run on circular tracks, rather than on straight courses or straightaways. Races run on straight courses are primarily those intended to establish speed records. However, the vast majority are conducted on tracks comprising of both straightaways and curves.

Many racing car enthusiasts share the consensus that attaining the highest levels of speed on a straightaway does not require much skill. They believe that a twelve year old could accomplish this task by simply depressing the accelerator of a racecar while keeping the vehicle within the lane. However, attempting to attain the highest levels of speed while negotiating tight turns on a racetrack with turns is another matter altogether. Let us discuss this for a moment.

Driving at high levels of speeds on a straightaway could be likened to idyllic experiences where life is uncomplicated and we are experiencing pure bliss.

However, along the course of life we will inevitably encounter treacherous curves that will subject us to painful episodes and shake the foundations of our existence. In the midst of our merriment while we are moving along in high spirits singing hallelujahs, some disturbing incident will roil our existence and throw us into a destabilizing curve. The question at this juncture becomes, "How should we react to curves?"

When professional drivers encounter curves, they instinctively downshift to a lower gear, in order to maintain control over the vehicle. But before exiting the curve on to the straightaway, they must first negotiate a critical part of the curve known as the *apex of the turn*. At this critical juncture, drivers employ a maneuver that might appear illogical to the average person. They accelerate and simultaneously shift to a higher gear. The G-forces operating on the vehicle causes its speed to increase exponentially, thereby generating higher exit speed as the vehicle is catapulted out of the turn onto the straightaway.

The vast majority of individuals have the tendency to apply brakes when life throws them into a curve of adversity and they eventually become immobilized by the besetting dilemma. Had they been aware of the truth that adversity need not have the last word and need not stop them in their tracks, they would be able to visualize a victorious outcome that is orchestrated by the power of God and thereby take the necessary actions to accelerate out of adversity. They would react like Paul and Silas did after they were imprisoned in a Philippian jail. Rather than applying brakes to their evangelistic endeavors, the two apostles engaged in praying and singing to God in the velvet darkness of midnight. They conducted a revival service even though they were imprisoned for doing the very same thing. In the midst of their prayers an earthquake erupted and shook the foundations of the prison, opening doors and loosening chains that held them captive.

Paul and Silas behaved like skilled drivers. Life had thrown them a painful curve and they were in the throes of a midnight situation. But because they were cognizant of the fact that God had the final word that dictated how their situation would ultimately turn out, they remained joyful. Rather than bemoan the adversity to which they were subjected, they offered up praise to God. Deep in a curve of adversity they intensified spiritual activity and God swung wide the prison doors and broke the fetters that held them captive (Acts 16:25-26).

The writer of Hebrew tells us that, "Faith is the substance of things hoped for, the evidence of things not seen" (Hebrews 11:1). God will never emplace us on a higher spiritual plane until such time that we are prepared to exercise faith and give him something to work with in those instances when we are subjected to midnight situations or find ourselves at the apex of life's challenging turns. He expects us to act the very way professional drivers do when they make critical adjustments to alter the performance of their vehicles, thereby resulting in greater exit speed when they hit the straightaway. This corollary is borne out by the example of Paul and Silas and the woman with the issue of blood. Neither individual permitted adversity to grind them to a standstill. Instead, they altered the spiritual climate of their existence by invoking the life-transforming powers of heaven, compelling God to respond and catapult them on a trajectory of liberation. Our heavenly Father expects each of His children to respond in like manner when we are confronted by a curve of adversity. He expects us to visualize victory by keeping our eyes on the checkered flag and intensify spiritual activity that will compel heaven to respond and catapult us unto the highway of freedom.

One of the most indispensable facets of automobile racing is the existence of pit stops. During competitive events drivers are afforded the opportunity to make intermittent stops to refuel depleted gas reserves, replace worn tires or undertake critical mechanical adjustments to their vehicles that would enable them to survive the long haul and possibly win the race. Also, when mechanical problems occur, drivers are compelled to engage in pit stops, in order to make necessary adjustments to their vehicle. But, as a preventive measure, drivers engage in intermittent stops to service their vehicles to forestall the occurrence of mechanical difficulties. By the same token, God requires that we engage in spiritual pit stops, in order to receive indispensable inputs to our spirit that would enable us avoid unnecessary blunders and continue our journey to the finish line of life.

Far too many individuals become spiritually fatigued to the point that they limp through life like automobiles that were involved in a serious mishap, suffered a blown engine or some other serious mechanical problem. They become worn down to the point that they lack the internal power capable of sustaining them at optimum levels of performance. They are dented and battered by adversity and eventually spin out of control and come to a complete stop. In the vast majority of cases these individuals have unwittingly contributed to their own undoing. While on life's straightaways experiencing mountain top experiences, they ignored the imperative of making necessary pit stops to engage in preventive maintenance to their spirit. As a result, when they were unexpectedly thrown into one of life's oppressive curves, they became devastated because they lacked the spiritual acumen that would have enabled them to respond adequately to the assault.

While in the spiritual arena the word "pit" conjures up negative images, when we employ the metaphor of an automobile race, it is not a bad place to visit. Pit crews are highly skilled personnel who provide indispensable support to drivers, such as changing tires in a matter of seconds, employing high-powered pumps to refuel vehicles in lightning speeds and making critical mechanical adjustments that would enable drivers to complete and possibly win their race. While it is the driver who is usually the "star" attraction and the one who invariably receives adulation after crossing the finishing line to take the checkered flag, they could never win any race without the support of expert pit crews.

Making pit stops to engage in preventive maintenance might entail taking time out of hectic study and work schedules to attend workshops, retreats, conferences, or engage in some other activity that would serve to enhance our spiritual growth and build us up to withstand the painful curves of life. It might even mean emulating the example of our Lord by frequently retreating to some isolated place to commune with our heavenly Father. It could further mean attending weekly prayer meetings or Bible sessions to replenish depleted energies between Sunday services. There are many activities one might engage in as a pit stop to nurture their spirit and provide them with the fortification to joyfully continue life's race.

Jesus was the expert when it came to making spiritual pit stops. His approach to life enabled him to keep his eyes on the prize and move up life's road with joy, despite the painful curves that were thrown his way. Because the Holy Spirit fortified him with power, he did not limp through life half-heartedly and at no time was he bitter about his lot in life, nor was he consumed by despair over unfair treatment that was constantly meted out to him by implacable enemies. He never lost hope, nor was he fearful about confronting his impending death. By engaging in spiritual maintenance, he was buoyed by joy for living.

Life has the tendency to beat and batter us by throwing unimaginable curves into our path. But by submitting ourselves to preventive maintenance — by making necessary pit stops as our Lord did, we will be able to function at a high state of spiritual readiness that will propel us across the finish line. Additionally, by making necessary pit stops, professional drivers indicate that they are committed to the race. By making spiritual pit stops we will likewise demonstrate that we are committed to completing the race that our heavenly Father has set before us.

As alluded to earlier, pit crews consist of highly skilled diagnosticians who provide invaluable support to professional drivers. However, many individuals live in a state of denial and feel that they could make it through the race of life under their own power. The truth of the matter is that we all need help at some point of our journey along life's road. There might be occasions when we *need* to consult with experts who could provide us with sage counsel that would enable us to increase our level of performance. We all have emotional blind spots and are not usually aware of those negative aspects of ourselves that some skilled diagnostician might see and it is by talking with them that we receive illumination into the way we operate. By consulting with a pastor, a therapist, or some other professional who possess expert knowledge that might enable us to recognize behavioral aspects that tend to impede our performance, we might be able to move up to a higher level of expertise. This is oftentimes a difficult step for many of us, even some professionals, because we do not easily open up to scrutiny and mistakenly assume that we possess all the answers to our problems and could make a go of things on our own. Jesus had twelve disciples and did not attempt go it alone. He utilized a pit crew to assist him in his endeavors and so should we.

Another exciting facet of automobile racing is the fact that winners celebrate after races. They ritualistically shake bottles of champagne, squirting the expensive beverage into the air and over everyone in close proximity to demonstrate their exhilaration about winning. However, God does not want us to wait until we get to heaven to celebrate. **He wants us to celebrate life in the here and now!** He wants us to be joyous **NOW!** He wants us to take time out of our busy schedules to play. Playing is an essential ingredient in remaining joyful throughout one's lifetime. Engaging in leisure time activities alone or with family members is good medicine for the soul, because it takes us away from stress-filled schedules of "producing" and affords us the opportunity to recharge our emotional and spiritual batteries. It affords us the opportunity to decompress from the debilitating tensions of daily living and allow our systems to rejuvenate.

Scores of individuals involved in important endeavors that make meaningful contributions to life are oftentimes miserable and experience very little or no joy, because they forgot how to play. They take everything in life so seriously that they eventually lose their sense of humor. **Humor is one of the soul's weapons in the battle for self-preservation.** It is a well known fact that humor, more than anything in the human make-up can afford us an aloofness and the ability to rise above any stressful situation, even if only for a few seconds. Our heavenly Father is desirous that we take time out of our hectic schedules to be humorous — to play.

Another aspect of automobile racing is the fact that professional drivers are masterful at effectively utilizing the terrain. They economize energy by refraining from excessively shifting their vehicles erratically from side to side and maintain straight-line trajectories when they are not negotiating turns. Invariably, it is not the driver with the fastest car that usually crosses the finish line to take the checkered flag, but one who in addition to engaging in skillful driving, employs aerodynamic techniques that demonstrate mastery over the course. For example, by drafting behind another car, a driver could conserve energy and at just the right moment move from behind the car they were using as a draft vehicle and slingshot to the head of the pack to cross the finish line. In other words, expert drivers know how to "work" the track in order to win. They do not amass knowledge of aerodynamics and the terrain for its own sake. Instead, they acquire and employ such knowledge to catapult them into the winners' circle! By the same token, God expects us to "work" His word, in order to fight the good fight and be catapulted into the winners' circle of life. Isaiah declares, "No weapon formed against thee shall prosper" (Isaiah 54:17). It is by "working" God's word in the curves of life that we experience His succor and support and realize that He will never leave us, nor forsake us. By "working" His word we petition His Spirit to take residence within our spirit, whereby we become infused with a confidence that enables us to look out on life with eyes of joy.

In describing his mission statement to planet earth Jesus declared, "I come that ye might have life and have it more abundantly" (John 10:10b). God is not desirous that we go through life spiritually impaired and performing at levels far below our created potential. He is desirous that we participate fully in our earthly pilgrimage by partaking of His *shalom* — His all-around goodness and harmony for our lives. He wants us to experience life as a cheerful adventure and one of POWER. This is the truth that is shed abroad in our hearts when our heavenly Father gives us beauty for ashes and turns our mourning into dancing and enlightens us to the reality of our belovedness. With the dawning of this reality our spirit become energized and rise up in a sacred doxology, acknowledging that a new and joyous awareness has been bestowed upon us — an awareness announcing that nothing shall separate us from the love of God. This heavenly echo reverberating in our spirit makes us the recipients of morning joy.

Weeping may endure for the night but joy comes in the morning (Psalm 30:5).

Order Form

To order additional copies, fill out this form and send it along with your check or money order to:

Amazing Grace Publications
P.O. Box 69
Van Brunt Station
Brooklyn, NY 11215
Cost per copy $15.95 plus $3.00 P&H.
Ship _____ copies of *Joy Cometh in the Morning* to:

Name_____

Address:_____

City/State/Zip:_____
___ Check for signed copy

Please tell us how you found out about this book.
___ Friend   ___ Internet
___ Book Store ___ Radio
___ Newspaper ___ Magazine
___ Other _____